FLOORS OF ENDURING BEAUTY

Other Publications by Steve Venright

The Illustrated Venright English Dictionary (illustrated by William Davison & Sherri Lyn Higgins; BookThug, 2004)

The Sleepy Turbine (illustrated by Kerry Wright Zentner; LyricalMyrical, 2003)

Spiral Agitator (Coach House Books, 2000)

A Neureality (Martin Garth Press, 2000)

Rotatiga Larips (THE EXPERT PRESS, 2000)

The Long & the Short of It (Letters, 1999)

Straunge Wunder (illustrated by Richard Kirk; Tortoiseshell & Black, 1996)

Notes Concerning the Departure of My Nervous System (Contra Mundo Press, 1991)

Visitations (Underwhich Editions, 1986)

For Chrissi & Jordan
Hope you find these floors up to scratch!
Fond good wishes, Steve

FLOORS OF ENDURING BEAUTY

STEVE VENRIGHT

Mansfield Press

Copyright © Steve Venright 2007
All rights reserved
Printed in Canada

Library and Archives Canada Cataloguing in Publication

Venright, Steve
    Floors of enduring beauty / Steve Venright.

Poems.
ISBN 978-1-894469-33-3

    I. Title.

PS8593.E58F56 2007   C811'.54   C2007-906104-4

Editor for the Press: Stuart Ross
Cover Design: Mansfield Creative
Cover Photo: Steve Venright
Typesetting: Stuart Ross

The publication of *Floors of Enduring Beauty* has been generously supported by
The Canada Council for the Arts and
The Ontario Arts Council.

Mansfield Press Inc.
25 Mansfield Avenue, Toronto, Ontario, Canada M6J 2A9
Publisher: Denis De Klerck
www.mansfieldpress.net

to
Mom & Dad
with love

CONTENTS

The Turbulated Curtain
9

One Hundred and Seventeen Steps to Instant Gratification
31

Six Epistles
36

Frickitt's Curve
44

Beautiful Thoughts
46

Afternoon of the Needle Gnomes
58

The Tin of Fancy Excrements: A Journey of the Self
59

Distended Aphorisms
72

Manta Ray Jack and the Crew of the Spooner
74

THE TURBULATED CURTAIN

Part One
The Outside World

A COOL MORNING WITH FOSSILIZED LIGHT breathes a vapourized tincture of charred driftwood and damp underbellies into this attic cathedral where skin grows on walls and little children never visit, except perhaps in advanced stages of dream. The sloped stucco ceiling breeds demented visions that charge the nerves and saturate the religious parts of the brain.

Galaxies of dust—the floating skin!—swirl and collide like stoned traffic cops and lobotomized ballerinas, some with tiny planets circling their stars.

Now the room disappears and is replaced by a lake, or perhaps two lakes occupying the same space, both bottomless and neither with a shore. It is here that I will spend the rest of my days, sitting on a coloured ridge of thought, sniffing the turquoise water for traces of a woman I once knew, and, eventually, just out of habit.

IN A BLAZE OF CHOCOLATE the wood nymph hurtles through the office tower, exciting tensions and defoliating zeitgeists. We follow her with remote-control cameras, down to where the grocers lay their eggs. It's a creaky salvation for one who held the floor with quicksilver statuary not months before the arrest of those vile homespun corporate marauders.

I look out from a static breeze and catch a glimpse of hell: trowelled sarcophagi unlit in the sulphurous dawn, pricks hanging out at the stock exchange, overpriced steamed zucchini. All I want is to bark my dogs and call it a day. But the foam is up to my ankles now, and the clouds are down to my neck. I can hear the police in the alley crying out for sleep. It's a good sound.

A LANGUID LINGUAL TORRENT coming out of my own head like textoplasm, full of typogres and lexichauns. The day when a grainy velvet hum fell across the front lawn. Wolves seen only by children seen only by ghosts sauntered through the afternoon subdivision. Then a sun vent opened and dissolved time, as you may have heard.

Here comes another Ice Age flashback and a lost page from some fool's doctoral thesis about the use of prepared horseradish to treat esophageal dysfunction in razorback pigs. Veiny roots encased in clear ice. Elsewheres of rocket ships and painted lips and gleaming ledgers. Suntan oil and tarnished cigarettes, greasy mood fragments and sticky tortoiseshell spoon handles, dog syrup, all swirling now, all fermenting. Watch!

INTANGIBLE FLUFF DRIPPING from the fenders of abandoned dream cars in sunlit fields. Tendrils of blue sphagnum drop from the sky, spiralling downward with all the grace of a dyspeptic stockyard weasel shaver. This day was going to be special, but now it just seems like all the rest: a tin can rusting on a stump behind a shack inside the lobby of a Ludwig Mies van der Rohe bank tower populated by screaming armies of brokers and martial arts saleswomen. Still, we must make a go of it: there's a lot to be done and I can't waste my time writing about every little thing that happens.

SOOT-COVERED CAVERNS SO SOFT to the touch. Their snug arteries lead from the main gallery, whose pugnant orange light graces our faces and the faces of the dogs, too (all of which are scared shitless, though we ourselves are superbly tranquil). That tubular hallway over there loops around that other hallway, and I wouldn't be surprised if that loft-like aperture is somehow connected to them both.

The sound of water from a distant stream—or near, perhaps—is so muffled it sounds like cotton strands being pulled delicately through a wound. What kind of natural factory is this? Nature's always up to something—always manufacturing life forms and surfaces. And maybe this is beside the point, but I think we could float down that tunnel over there if we tried. It's just a feeling, but it's worth a shot. Say goodbye to our bosses, our ministers, our parole officers and just float like a couple of dandelion puffs (I mean, we'll say goodbye to them in our heads—no need to go back to the parking lot). Then we'll drift weightless through the coiling soot tunnels of this inartificial place, this little transmutopia, ready to screech in surprise at what we might find, or just twirl and...sleep.

A QUIET DAY WITH DOGS and skulking owls. Tinkling fists of aluminum talismans dangling down the breakfast shafts. Or enamelled rosewood cubes not meant for touching.

There are worlds of quiet majesty beyond this reality, each one successively more horrifying. The last one is a galactic jack-in-the-box that erases our memory with terror and sends us back to the start.

POWDERLESS TERRACOTTA CURLICUES are woven inside the skull, making these dead groundhogs more than just tea room paperweights, items of feigned curiosity. A man sits writing in a small booth charmingly prattled with alabaster and mahogany. There's a blue tint to how stupid that seems. Years from now he'll probably still be sitting there, writing away like a buffoon about god-knows-what—frost or something, probably.

THERE IS FROST ON THE GLASS statues of copulating humans in the courtyard of the litigation emporium. There is frost on the wings of dead bumblebees, and frost on the crotches of trees where messed-up squirrels slumber haphazardly. On the windows of condemned infirmaries: frost. On the caps of dozing lobster fishermen vacationing in the interior: frost. There is even frost on the sawdust piled up outside the corner slaughterhouse. The frost is composed of an infectious pattern of tiny crystals, each bearing a microscopic schematic for a device that can turn crayfish shells into wallpaper. That's just a guess, but at least I'm trying to make sense of this ostensibly demented infestation of frozen translucence. Nature seldom acts without purpose—we just have to look very closely to reveal its motives, to decipher its often peculiar gists. Farmers have always known this. That's why you'll sometimes see one bent over a wayward grouse with a hand mirror, or rubbing a cow's spittle between his coarse hands until it dries up or, on rare occasions, catches fire. That's why they're friends with witches.

SICK TWISTING SULLAGE GURGLING down the promenade, swirling like the fouled expectations of a beribboned little girl. Fatuous blaring detritus flapping through cannibal-mirrored laundry chutes where rheumatic old retrievers tangled in sheets might easily be caught, snagged voiceless in perpetuity. Stark nauseous whimsy, putrescent glee, respiring with sudden hate at the recognition of vicious tricks.

The process of transformation is likely to be a long one, absent some catastrophic and catalyzing event....

A candy store of dust and mould and dry squalid sunbeams heaving daftly onto the brainless, idiotic linoleum of its floor.

"I'm sorry, it's all gone."

Grey walls where proud parcels in colourful wrappers once boasted distinctive and highly desirable regalities and brazen ecstasies.

"No, I'm sorry, there's nothing left, little fellow. It's the end of the world and all the sweets have dried up and blown away. No more candy ever. I'm just here to close up shop. Don't be sad."

And the walls start to crumble. Poofing cloudlets of plaster gasps whiffling from the moronic structure. A cyclone of desiccated dreams calls itself forth but dissipates before any useful damage is done. The worst thing would be to leave this place standing, a monument to innocent exploding desire never to be satisfied. And the radio sings: *There'll be a place for us—somewhere a place for us....*

A GROGGY VELVET SMOKE snips its way across the receding glandular churchyards of a silent mid-morning town that smells softly of fish heads and embroidered driftwood. Old tomcats lie dead or sleeping on corroding cedar porches, the news seeping grimly or waltzing rabidly into their skulls from a publishing factory a few kilometres away. The throats of grackles and frogs alike are silent this morning, as are the giant slugs that scrape along the ochre asphalt of the town square. It is there that the bloodthirsty, oafish and voyeuristic sun dumps its ambrosial rays, ensieved, through the hairy weft of smoke as it tickles the flags of shopfronts in its dubious languid lurk across a town best forgotten, best left unvisited by rovers such as us.

And so we go back to our little submarine, waiting with timid sharks near the naked though gauzy beach. It's the most snake-ridden beach in the province, according to our guidebook, but we don't see a single one. Ghost planes fly above the dirty green sea. A panther lopes about in a lonesome meander a little ways down the shore, lost in thought or waiting for something that seems never to happen.

How I'd love to sleep now, but there will be plenty of time to nap when we get beneath the waves again. The purple smog from sandy bones invades our sinuses, makes us think of the old times, and we go.

Part Two
The Golden Age of Noxious Drivel

SILVERY DRIBBLES ON PINK WOOD make a lasting impression. The forecast is glim, but as you walk across the fissured cinnamon tarmac, remember: wildlife clothes itself, in fur, feather and flower. Do the same and you will be admitted into the secret society of wombats, goldfinches and daffodils.

The lawlessness of the countryside—with all its dells and thistles—has appalled many an innocent traveller. Woe unto him who has run out of gases on some godforsaken stretch of pastoral resplendence. Who will rescue the lost post-urbanite? This and other unanswerable questions will be the focus of our next daytime edition of *Get That Thing Off Me*. Please join us next week when our guests will include a woman who forgot to name her children and a man who despises ocelots. Until then, this is unoccupied mental territory without boundaries or defences, held up by crutches in a dim region of sanctified nothingness. You have only yourselves to blame, and the people around you, and a few who couldn't make it for medical reasons, along with your ancestors and, I might suggest, their enemies.

Please stay tuned for *The Farm Report.*

NOW YOU TOO CAN wake up screaming for joy each morning, thanks to the patented new Regalsheath Toothpick Holder™. The Regalsheath Toothpick Holder safely and conveniently stores as many as three dozen toothpicks for up to two hundred years! Don't die unfulfilled, like your neighbour down the street and Amelia Earhart—get the Regalsheath Toothpick Holder today! Buy two and we'll throw in one reusable weather-resistant hypoallergenic Dr. Hobagobulgis Aluminum Toothpick™ at no extra charge! (Must be of legal age. Manufacturer not liable for injuries resulting from misuse.)

HERE IS YOUR PRAIRIE of voices, with stripes that excite. Furry skyscrapers stand camouflaged in wheatfields. Farmers circumnavigate them in combines at night—deep silent night where the dead thrive. But this is no subject for a snowy urban afternoon. Let's talk about the woodgrain of floorboards and fluid dynamics instead. And squid, if you don't mind.

WOULD ANYONE LIKE A KICK in the side? With mellow café au lait rays pouring through the sheer drapes? On a cat's tongue magnified thirty times? In brittle, constipated, airless offices? Through dead-end streets where rebel lovers kiss the way unemployed astronauts sign petitions against crossword puzzles that are too hard for the elderly? Between wheatfields oozing with caramel and dead canaries? Over drinks at the Happy Crescent? Under cover of nightgowns and hotshot ratdogs, or cardboard boxes full of ice cubes? They pulverized the towers and they shot him in the limo and they got your sister hooked and they slaughtered all those farmers and they shredded up your ballot and they dropped some big white bombs and they jailed those kids for dreaming. At a tea room in the meadow on some diaphanous afternoon? Around a tapestry of hoofprints on a snowy frozen lake? For the rockets made of blue rubber and Aztec codices? Into nothing but fluffy beige garages with arcing stellar sparks?

SOMEONE TOLD YOU it was going to be easy. Your houseguests would not oversleep or get crumbs in the honey. Crazy rich men in caves halfway around the planet would not magically disable your entire air defence system. Women would not recoil at the sight of your shoes. Stained plaster gable walls would not speak to your visual cortex in the pictorial language of Lucifer, making you see things even after you close your eyes. You would not experience terrible guilt at the suffering of your neighbours down the street and across the globe—suffering worse than even your occasional insomnia, aversion to pink on tan and lactose intolerance. Massive fractal formations would not flatten your crop fields, appearing so swiftly and mysteriously at midday there are no culprits to sue. Porn-sniffing horses mounted by cops would not regularly misidentify the contents of your satchel, they would not stare into your watery eyes and bare their fangs. Tightrope-walking buskers would never fall to the pavement when you were on duty. You would not be called upon to sex at a glance so many androgynous customers. Your UFOs would not all turn out to be weather balloons, Venus or migraine phosphenes. No one would berate your self-conscious dog for its haircut. Your phonograph would not leak. Dead relatives, visiting unseen with counsel from beyond the veil, would not spy on your undignified secret recreations. Your stream of consciousness would not be full of leeches that latch on to the underside of helicopters airlifting gangrenous sea lions to Satanic veterinary clinics in the heart of the Congo while Neanderthal mermaids play Russian roulette with poisonous vipers singing snippets from *Carmina Burana* on an island in the antipodes of your mind. No one would tell you that you look great when they're obviously just saying it because you look so awful. The wind would not whisper its epithets to everyone but you. Third-rate poets would not scoff at your lack of character, you spineless automaton. False blips would not distractingly appear on your radar screen. At least no one told you it wasn't going to be difficult.

WHAT HOPE IS IN A DROP OF RAIN GLIDING down a woman's sternum? What hope is in a snowflake melting on a dead man's tattooed ankle? Science and mathematics alone cannot answer these questions. They must be married to philosophy and religion before a true analysis is possible. There are those who think the only way to close a door is by sliding on their belly across the floor until enough pressure is effected that the door becomes no longer open. Others think the opposite—but is either notion correct? If you put a dog in heat does it become a scorpion? That would be like tying two chickens together and calling it a bell. It's not rocket surgery. All you need is a strong belief in something other than common sense: for example, the Golden Age of Steam Engines, or how to repair a spoon drawer. Sometimes it seems there's just no proper way to end a discourse.

THE WOODS ARE FULL of chihuahuas. The grease from cocoons trickles down onto the tails of turkeys and the stubs of opera tickets. The pool of type dries up at the forward foot of a small blue panther. The peculiar cat sniffles and longs to wonder what an understanding of words is all about. Intelligence without language is entirely possible, but there are so many ways to speak the world. A tree speaks it with its bark. A cloud speaks it with its lack of residuals. No one understands less poorly than I the equivocal necessity of...silence.

And now for the weather.

A SUSTAINED BLEAR CASCADING down the terraced glottal dales. Overnight a probability of isolated mercurial contagions blossoming intermittently into patches of sustained libidinal envelopment. White-furred mammals are expected to occur eidetically across much of the southern frontier, heralding even more hysterical visions by mid-week. Transpersonal delusions will be developing right before our eyes in the form of a crusty appealing frost. Otherwise, the usual epidermal saturations, spinning reptile discs and rashes of domestic overfastidiousness can be expected until at least the weekend, when hedge nymphs with blowdarts endeavour to retake the suburban matrix.

Volunteer officers will again be patrolling the countryside in an attempt to break up any instance of wildlife copulation. Sticks and nets will be used, mace if necessary, little toothpicks and sticky rods for the fornicating insects, plumbing apparatus to shove down holes on hunches, laboratory-grown mucous membranes, terrier whips, whippet bats, bat radios, radio scarecrows, electronic lightning, vegetal moulds, slingshot dildos, parakeet hammers, glass taffeta feathers onions blood keys velum sacs glue hot water bottles woodchips.

GLISTENING FORMULAE written backwards and inside-out: second tree on the left, encircling the trunk at eye level, about three centimetres from the bark.

A forest without trees is not necessarily a room, just as a room without walls is not necessarily a forest. You can see whatever you like from wherever you may be. There are surfaces everywhere, if you look closely—surfaces upon surfaces: rashes of pseudo-sphagnum on sloped garret ceilings, shifting liquid crystal numerical codes on nipples and other glands, posters of perfect worlds on otherwise gloriously mundane subway platform walls. And then there's Ligeti's *Adaptations for Barrel Organ* eating through your mental curtains like a very pretty drunken scarab that's really hungry or something. Stuff grows on things decaying, and that's all I can really say about it at the moment. More on that sort of thing later.

I SEE SOMETHING packing itself into a Citroën, with gassy ligatures and shallow water tucked under infatuated seams. There are good-looking fish here and scapular glissandos fighting to free us from the white and silver dome. Mouth scaffolding appears in rogue outcroppings pulled into night like a magician's handkerchief through an unclosed wound arriving in 1982 or thereabouts.

So your theory was true: it is possible to cakewalk without hydroscopes; it is possible to scour the faucets without using animal products. And why would we want to buy animal products when we can support our own economy? Let's proceed based on the hypothesis that certain frequencies can slump through unplunged slivers of crawling solar flares. Nothing would change—you and I would still be represented by ciphers, there would still be trashy hoards of dizzy bards dashing abroad aboard dachshunds on dashboards flashing forward into new upheavals, new revelatory quests, new standard effects.

Sir, the plane is now ten miles out. Does the order still stand?

Anything begets everything. The voices in the background are part of the music. The ticket booth is part of the performance. The war is an advertisement. Whitewashed hells burn through our wires like a vain model, an architectural template of ovoid steel. The noise behind the curtain is part of the tour. Let it guide you down poured concrete chasms into the secret lush interior of the soft core populated by gorgeous demons who couldn't care less about you. Let it take the form of a rococo cocoon, a crinkled origami raccoon that bites at your postulations and frivolously entices porcupines the size of the moon held out at arm's length. Thus will you be led into the antechamber. A moiré eel. Start to chop it into pieces with your tongue. They will arraign you according to sighs.

SHE SCREAMS HERSELF TO SLEEP each night in a white tide pool on the outskirts of town. During the day she's a receptionist for a mock pharmaceutical company called Fine Persian Drugs. Her only living uncle is famous for being able to contact the gods. No one knows this, except for us, but he once made love with a dolphin. The dolphin spoke of this communion to her friends, who were always amused by her sexual exploits with lower life forms.

IN OTHER NEWS, the Ancient Ones have returned, and they're as deranged as can be. We'll have a full report on that after this week's episode of *The Elegant Spirals of Slime Mould Amoebas.* Archaic Revival Time begins tonight, so remember to set your clocks back 18,000 years. The sun is expected to rise in the east tomorrow but it will sink in the west, contrary to our earlier report. And those little feathery things flying through the air that everybody's been so concerned about? Don't be alarmed—they're birds, a kind of airborne vertebrate descended from dinosaurs. Our network palaeontologists say they're harmless unless seriously provoked, in which case they may attack the elderly, children and single male office workers between the hours of 4 and 6 p.m. when they're most vulnerable.

We'll return in one form or another after this message.

THE BEST ELEVEN MINUTES of your life await you at Blackdale Orchards. *(Cue: Pachelbel's Canon at triple speed)*

AS THE BRAIN IS TO CONSCIOUSNESS what the horse is to its rider and the bonfire to a hobo, so the scorpion is to water sports what the Milky Way is to the rectum and that's of no interest to you so just close your eyes and open your mouth and keep walking until you don't hit anything.

Scritch scritch. Nighttime. A human mother crying in her sleep. A long-lost dead forgotten dream washed up on her neighbour's lawn by mistake. Nothing to reclaim those days with—not even nights. A sheep that slits up the gravelled weave of hair: what we all confess to wanting without admitting it.

And now, our day's work done, we turn our thoughts to chewy primeval things that bring us comfort in the back seats of our white cadillacs and, I think I'll say, in our unspeakable confectionery needs.

THIS SUDDEN TREE, this popular socket, white-haired along the periphery where clouds are the loudest. The sun smothers another lake with its black glow. Desolate underwater sex and, reflected in the sky, flotillas of warrior canoes (which often double in dreams as happily invading starships).

Here is where you took me to drown or to baptize me, but instead we sit shooting skeet on docks made of purple rubber. Ants the size of small insects eat our lunch.

WE ARRIVED BY TRAIN at a strange city, similar in every way to the one we'd departed. We kept writing down your name so we wouldn't...well, we wouldn't forget it, but just to be on the safe side we wrote it on plastic walls in sleet and we wrote it on police cruisers in dog breath and we wrote it on tree limbs in starlings and we were by then transuding obscenely so we had to go to one of those government gymnasiums for swingers—they've got a hose and you spray each other up and down even in places you didn't know you had: extra upper lips, Edwardian dewlaps, underscalps, reserve sphincters, curving dorsal ridges, third eyes, marsupial pouches (on some of the women), external genitalia, forests, valleys, entrance ramps onto the Don Valley Parkway, scruffy canine outgrowths and things we don't normally talk about at the dinner table, even when entertaining a dead thistle like you.

A THIN, ICY CRUST OF SNOW cloaks the observatory. Fawns nibble tax receipts and candlesticks in the faux forest.
    They took out the heart, they were all ready to transplant it, and they forgot completely what they were doing. Not just how to do it, but they didn't even have a clue suddenly who they were or, as stated previously, what they were doing. Remarkably, the patient from whom the heart had been taken lived while the would-be recipient, not surprisingly, did not.
    And now a word from our sponsor.

YOU'LL CERTAINLY LOOK A TERROR in this horrible new spherical sidewinder snake-missile jacket displacer that makes the same snap you get when a door closes unexpectedly on your principal divestitures. There are motherless flags, there are insensate tensile stencils, there are... The list goes on, but best of all there are *timeless elegances*. Each box of Piffle™ has a little piece of timeless elegance taped discreetly to the inside of its hindquarters. Your friends will never know the difference!

THERE ARE PLENTY OF CRACKS IN THE SQUALL that go all the way down to the grey stone bridge with twinkling crescents. An aura of fog dogs the hogs as they clamber over the arch, looking for bells they've been taught to seek.

Meanwhile, you, or someone representing you, undergo brooding crenellations while I read from Coleridge in the corner. It's nothing new, I just haven't mentioned it till now.

My ego has dispersed too soon: I have nothing with which to replace it. Hence, the vacuity of these lines.

SHE REALLY GETS MY DONKEYS up onstage. I love the way she plays with their expectations, like a little dragon-faced hen bursting with tinsel and frayed at the wrong end.

Will this hour never end? It's the same as all the others but it seems to be caught on something.

THE FLOWER OPENS like a bad play. The quail is as sad as can be, which is perhaps not very sad at all, but still it tortures my soul to see it thus. And the blasted demolition work going on outside my window keeps threatening to wake me as I write these lines to you—you whom I've always trusted with my favourite bottle-cleaning brush.

Speaking of which, what do *you* think happened to World Trade Centre 7?

WHAT'S LEFT BUT THESE SHUDDERING GEARS of flesh, ratcheting on towards indifferent death? Famines and wars and cyclones and epidemics and genocides and earthquakes, and still their visceral grind rumbles valiantly, dorkishly, beneath the cold stars whose ancient illusory light sparkles in a false heaven. Quickly now, while there's still hope, let us rape the planet, let us murder the future and... Oh, never mind, you don't want to hear about such things. Back to our story!

THE NEWSPAPERS IN THOSE DAYS heralded the return of the blood-red raven, a bird whose feathers were indeed blood-red and strikingly brilliant, though some were an orangey-red, a sort of Italian red, and when seen together the two tones of this elite ornithological anomaly produced in humans a giddiness and awe followed immediately by a hapless despair ofttimes leading to clumsy impromptu suicide attempts.

The last thing you ought to know about that era is that everyone—even horse-racing jockeys and ministers—wore sickly pastel plaids. Things, in my opinion, got much better a few years later, when the women of cutting-edge fashionable mien revolted by wearing solid fuchsias and corals with lapis details and silver accessories and began sporting artificial moustaches. I may not be a fashion critic, but I know what I like.

AND NOW, HERE IN THE PRESENT, small monsters churn our dreams into clotted froth.

We see maps of Hell in lucent furs, with lines tangled around our indemnities. Catching fish with brassieres, trolling on lakes that are "the counterfeit of death." I look up at Mars and scream, for I shall inhabit the universe and my soul is a radiant pig that lives on without me, going where I'd never go.

That's not news, but that too is reality.

CRUTCH-LIKE EXCRESCENCES and diaphanous furniture bleeding orange from the torso. A gown of wood embarking on a dream into the savage mist. And that headless thought on the horizon, ever stable in its quarantine. A night to remember. Even totemic beetle-pillars come out to play as the terrestrial feathers crawl through Silurian dunes of grey and purple. You will always be special to me, even when I cease to exist. And when I am no longer here, I want you to call my name every third Monday through the globular fields, a fragrant ochre horror umbralizing your face.

Primordial cityscapes in golden reds and rich excremental browns slosh past our visual plane to left and right. Deeper we go into the present. Deeper into the forbidden present. A chaos of perception and we're into the pure land. Soft and sharp and viscid, we fall into its morphic lust with abandon. There'll be nothing left but the bones, such clean and lovely bones, such tranquillizing bones. They weft us into future life through murky plateaux, melting diluvial vistas. Unbroken dreams.

Part Three
The Sleepy Turbine

THERE'S A SEVEN-POINTED STAR above her head, but don't let that put you off. A hundred years from now, no one will remember whether you entered cinemas from the right or the left. All they'll care about is whether the octopus was actually flying or whether you threw it.

Out here in the shaggy twilight we waltz sombrely beside Shiva-blue plaster walls cut into the... How can I explain this? The hills rise just above our heads. They've been cut away vertically to provide an interconnected series of courtyards. The excavated surfaces have been thickly plastered in a sort of bumpy adobe fashion. The plaster has been dyed dusty blue, verging on violet.

But now the scene changes. A parlour during wartime. Woodgrain on every surface, so enfolded as to convolute the bounds of vision. Everything is seeing us, and we are absorbed.

In these moments when we forget to gasp, out comes a bilious undersea life form from our glottal apertures. It says something about the way we lead our lives, always perpendicular to the gnawing wave of externality, governed as it is by fixed resources.

HWY. 401 IS MOVING WELL BEYOND ISLINGTON
AND OUT INTO THE STARS

HIS PRINCELY JUICE FOR NIGHTMARES, and a pliant rumba flux hovering between the glass braids and the sticky torsion fibres. It is a world now glowing with xylophonic tumescence, supreme and crustaceous—a little white meat from the steamed brains of hand-fed panthers or beagles. They start the cessation here, where all the grown men cry their various wares. Something like a stuffed trumpet—a gas sunhorn?—can be heard. Vacuum-packed pig hearts are bazookaed into the bay or through the windows of twelfth-storey furriers and black-market hatters. Illegal swamp games can be imagined, even where signs warn against dog-teasing. As the afternoon turns to midnight, I sweep you into my arms and address you civilly, if not correctly.

THIS ONE GETS A KNIFE right through the neck, thanks to some squiddish rat-thing hiding beneath the table as he hangs upside-down doing bad unlucky yoga in the Boschean superfurnace. The spongy groves are dank, welcoming of large abnormal fish, and we go there without hope of return. Trickling water on moss makes us shudder cozily. The moon comes up green and scares us half to death. Meanwhile, there's a wedding in which the bride is being eaten by two-legged seals with horrible fangs, and everyone present—priest and groom included—is transfixed by a feeling of terror and anguish arising directly from observation of this atrocity. A heavy white vapour blows in from the sea and envelops first the church, then the whole town, in its milky suffocating shroud. The organist plays on: morosely sweet hymns distended and contorted by the frightful murky circumstances.

Let us crawl over the damp grasses till we reach the cliff. There, looking down, we will stare jealously at the dreary cavortings of fisherfolk on the beach far below.

I STRETCH THE JUNGLE. I pummel the grottoes. I pluck the sounds of shifting earth. I remove the clouds with a wave of my goblet. I unstring the horses and the corpses of the grove. I embitter the children in their dreams. I siphon the bees. I defenestrate the pyroglyphic carpets. I smush the waterfalls. There is a greenly glowing figure above the cove. I listen the air out of rabbits. I decouple the goblins. I shatter the breezes. Long flowing velvet discharge of the amniotic galaxies. I uncrunch the windows. I hypnotize the puddles and their golden flapping carp. I dream the eels from the floorboards. I deface the wind. I impregnate selected seascapes. I soothe myself through mountains. Postcards of jackal gods rotting from the sky. I enlustre nuptial torsos. I breathe leopardskin onto glaciers and slow the ages. I bluster the sap already dripping. Black soggy trees. I untangle the worlds.

DREAMY SUCTION AND CLEAR spineless liquid delight. A phase-shifting cellular drone reaching out across even the secret meadows. In a purple custard innocence, gliders drift above your nakedness. The avenue is empty of people, its subterranean furnaces promising more than the afternoon can divulge. Water lapping on stones and flesh, a kiss under the vines, and everyone disappears from thought save for the conjoined entities, of which you are one.

POOLS OF IVORY AND TURQUOISE fluid. Birds breaking up into fluff beneath the eclipse. Once you start to fall, everything sparkles and explodes quietly. The valley detonates itself for your diversion (you are suspended high up and to the east). A powdery sense of déjà vu soon forgotten as you turn your thoughts to the anointed fur of the one beside you.

SLICING through the aluminum dome, we find a blue windy softness within, and it is the blue windy softness of a certain 1957. Vintage exotica suspended in virtual sonic formaldehyde. Night erupts upon suppuration of the shell: absolute dymaxion perfection, but with a tincture of quasi-Incan sultry salaciousness for good measure and arousal. And then a howling tubular bell eventually disrupts the gentle confusion.

IT'S A TERRIBLE THING, HAVING TO TRAWL through all these life forms until you find one that resembles you. But beyond the almost palpable rupture of days so horrible lies a greedy tranquillity that sucks at our endorsements and sends us off to bed before noon, where storybook daydreams plunge us into cat-tongued shivers and languid drool. A fever dismantles everything before our very eyes. Tiny death is still the darkest. But we won't think of that. Think instead of an unbridled ride on the bare backs of sedated zebras. Think of the chemical state of sleep, which scientists now say is capable of knitting up the ravelled sleeve of care, but only if you indulge in it with a wild primal abandon, engines black with desire, skirts fluttering and eyes wide. Delirium hatcheting into slumber. Pull the torpid curtains on this afternoon's repose and moisturize into a firming glow.

NERVES TURN TO POWDER here—didn't anyone mention?—but there's a silken jelly you can use that gets them back to almost normal. They sell it down at the wildlife organarium behind the prison. It's good for sliding scales, too.

ON THIS NIGHT THE COWS sleep more deeply than usual. The ice cubes are melting in my nightcap. A lodge is being demolished. What else? Oh yes: when I said there were things I hadn't told you, I was lying to conceal a deeper truth.

This is the ditch where everything coalesces into pure burning senseless reason. It's my sanctuary and it's sinking with a grim dissonant beauty. Your forgiveness is like a new egg to me. I jump on it from the overpass.

THEY PUT UP FALSE ARCHWAYS to scare the horses. They also offer prizes for loud lovemaking in tombs.

My current theory is that something crawled up into the motor and died there.

HOW CAN YOU MISTAKE A SPARK for a turtle? That's what I want to know. How can you startle a fish with a story about a pigeon, especially if you've never seen a pigeon before and the fish is a thousand or more kilometres away? These are the issues we'll face in the coming days. We'll need all our powers of reasoning and intuition. We'll need a hefty budget. But what we don't need are scientists giving us the answers. A lot of us will be falling into hedges—that has been prophesied by all the major religions. That is why we must rid ourselves of either hedges or religions. And which, in your real mind, would you rather have?

SUPERNATURAL FORCES IN A JUNGLE environment suit me just fine. All my friends are interconnected by a shimmering teleneural lattice I haven't told them about yet. I have taught the raccoons to wash my hair and groom my beard. In return I prepare them lavish culinary sculptures. The architecture of the city has attained consciousness. The birds sense this and are frightened, but the humans carry on oblivious to the change.

The massive obelisks have tottered and settled, leaning upon one another like curvy osseous shards, lovely in their windowless majesty. I'll climb that huge drumlin beside them to gaze again upon the concentric billows of its mown concavity. The slope is so steep I'll have to crawl up on my belly, but it will be worth the effort. A lawn like that, you normally see only in dreams.

THERE IS A WHITE STIFFNESS BREATHING out the murk from a sullen plethora of chapels in that same seaside town. A candy cane of moody regrets is what the fish are jumping for, right near the shore. Unbeknownst to us we walk in terry-cloth silence upon the sooty beach as the lighthouse bursts into artificial flame.

Please save these sailors, O wretched leviathan that lives within our dreams. They're decent pure souls who are in it just for the money, though they've every one come to love what they do. Let their bodies, if they must die, wash up to shore where we will mend their clothes and watch in talented horror as the locomotives roar right out of the waves and blast the beach with their predatory roar. Vicious radiance! The night collapses in our throats.

VICTORIAN HEDGES SEEN from a promontory. Gruff animals lurk, black-coated, as a carriage and a bicycle race to the death. There's an abundance of vanishing points: in fact, all the points seem to be vanishing, until we're left with only the rods and cones. The ivy, over verdigris, is so grey it camouflages the huge edifice at the end of the road—a palatial stone estate. Bears, we now see, have slunk out from the topiary gardens to eat away at the racing casualties. A sudden siren shoots silver sonic sabres into our soft sutured cerebrums, and then a different siren is heard—the siren reserved for air-raid alerts. The apiary explodes in anger. Those bears take heed and lift their bloody muzzles, sniffing at the sky and wagging their heads from side to side. A screaming metallic angel of death claws across the sky on its way to the designated kill zone. Chipmunks chitter as it passes. Groundhogs grit their teeth. And so the moral of the story is that anything can happen anywhere at any time, but those who are wise will be guided by instinct, desire and intuition, caring little for the vicissitudes of daily happenstance. Animals always go all the way, and settings transmute constantly.

SOME OF THE DRUNKEN SEISMOLOGISTS thought they might have accidentally killed a moose, whereas he's just posing in the mineral gallery with his juror's cap—one eye on the outside world, one eye on the crenellated ooze that remains unvacuumable.

Sitting on a terrace in France without benefit of seaways or arches, envious of men who kiss trophies in public. The news is all about a giant toad named Die Knoblauchrote—goes around eating owls that fall from trees after he hypnotizes them. A toddler on the tracks in a poster for the Sharpened Dance. You can't come within a mile of the smiling people without there being a chance operation. Is she a girl or a world or someone else's intention? Swans are screwing in the artificial pool. It's a closed system, enabling them not to die. It doesn't stop them from decaying, though. After several decades, you can imagine the state of their hair, not to mention the estate of their heir who went off and dyed a head of them. *There's a pretty face,* they'll say—*and she's a doctor of degeneration!* The speakers were all uninvited and none of them showed up. They blare their glockenhorns from the debts of their disparity, where no one else has been, save for the three goats watching television in the nude. Without benefit of spatial cognition, without recourse to freeways and sanitoriums, I no longer care about her perfect collarbones, her distinguished uvula, her incomparable noise floor.

THE CURTAINS ARE GETTING THIN at this edge of the world. The horses are squatting, backfiring and releasing their inner sanctums.

You cannot unhonk your horn, but you can unhook your pheasant, even if it's dead (in fact, it's easier that way). They come up from the earth looking famished and forgetful. Gears crumble and form anthills that would not look out of place in a fashionable hourglass. It's a strange way to tell the time but it's as good as any, I suppose. Devils are in the smoke. Clouds pump lavender into the graves, shooting streams of water with fish inside the conventional centre— as if you were leaking information into a calm pewter dish then splashing it all across the sky with a sad delight. They shine like oysters in orbituary columns connecting astral dots of constellations. Soon the night's canopy will be full and there'll be nothing left for us but cross words and prosy crocks of fiction. I can hardly believe how late it's getting—but then, the days are shorter every minute. It's just transition. Labour forces striking over contractions getting closer all the time coils into a ball of ire hissing venom through Venusian canals and beyond the pleated bleeding curtains into a new whirled orator's scream.

LIMPID SLOUGH—it's coming soon. Mark it on your calendar. Down all the hallways slowly tumbling forward in low corrugations. Badgers putrescing in the storm outside. Well, who ever heard of a storm inside, anyway. Music spilling flaccidly from belated winds.

There goes another crocodile. It's behind the stove. It will never know the joys of getting a driver's license or seeing its grandchildren walk the plank. A system of cloud promulgation has been set up to take our minds off this regrettable rumination. It would have worked a charm if we hadn't seen it coming. As subtle as a polka-dot tank on a moor. The gears that make our living room run glop together in an Arpy hump of waxen conglomorescence. So much for going out.

THE FREEWAYS ARE CLOGGED WITH SILVER flotsam, the clouds are jingling with lacquered froth, the bedrooms of the nation are frozen solid. This is no time to lapse into a woozy bloodless lassitude. There are animals without the least notion of who they are or why we're chasing them. A state of meaty bewilderment has been declared.

Are you prepared to succumb to minutiae? Or are you just bestride the geyser, dopily entranced? In either case we must ask you to return to your assigned position. The show is about to stop.

BETTER TO STRIKE WHILE STILL ASLEEP, in order to maintain an alibi. A cherubic barking up the wall loosens the paint enough that we can read the inscriptions underneath. However, we have discovered to our surprise and delight that we would rather just eat the paint as it peels away like the skin of a blank but meaning-filled chrysalis, the unscripted flesh of the years.... While out on the horizon an orange efflorescence continues to bloom and storm and calm the sway, grating on our invidious discomfiture like an undercooked malady greeping with slime. I cannot help but be enchanted by its malevolent charms: a thrashing contrapulition. It's beautiful and it's coming this way.

ONE HUNDRED AND SEVENTEEN STEPS TO INSTANT GRATIFICATION

1. Become sensitive to your environment.
2. Measure and analyze your current status.
3. Articulate the desired outcomes.
4. Eliminate all stress.
5. Give up expecting things from other people, or your life.
6. Install lights and switches to ensure all your stairways are well-lit.
7. Randomize your sensory inputs.
8. Exfoliate.
9. Record all the names you can think of on a sheet of paper and a brief note as to why you need to forgive them.
10. Write motivational texts on flashcards and stick them on your dashboard.
11. Encourage unrestricted breastfeeding.
12. Get your bunny used to being handled.
13. Focus on fruits.
14. See for yourself how your medication interacts with other drugs.
15. Prepare a checklist of the objects you might want to look at.
16. Always leave home well-groomed.
17. Check out the street conditions: is the pavement even?
18. Use a stick to check the firmness of the ground in front of you.
19. Know the warning signal and have a battery-powered radio.
20. Encourage earthworms and micro-organisms.
21. Find out what contaminants are in your local water supply and your home's water.
22. Recognize your tendency towards sin.
23. Fertilize naturally.
24. Always call local emergency personnel when someone is injured in an electrical accident.

25. Do a reality check.
26. Avoid being scalded by steam from a boiling pot.
27. Pare down the virus factor.
28. Encourage innovation by emphasizing small-scale technological solutions.
29. Know exactly how you feel about what happened and be able to articulate what about the situation is not okay.
30. Don't crowd around candidates who are seeking the Holy Ghost.
31. Use plenty of water.
32. Admit to another person in confidence, and in the presence of God, the exact nature of your faults.
33. Conquer procrastination.
34. Save major polishing for later.
35. Devise marketing strategies for your target market.
36. Don't tell traumatized people that they are "lucky it wasn't worse."
37. Develop a personal philosophy of time.
38. Install a firewall.
39. Identify not only your skills, but also your deepest values, interests and motivational preferences.
40. Sneeze into your elbow.
41. Learn to accept that your loss is real.
42. Recognize that positive change can be stressful and even frightening.
43. Flick switches with the side of your hand or wrist.
44. Be sure that your scissors are nice and sharp.
45. Tickle a baby.
46. Practice summarizing to a friendly colleague a paper you just read.
47. Avoid sharp corners on the ends of countertops, especially islands and peninsulas.
48. Implore the mercy of God by prayer and fasting.
49. Cover chicken parts in lemon juice.
50. Slim your silhouette.

51. If you find a wild animal in your home, do not trap or corner it.
52. Have eye contact, but don't stare.
53. Watch for sod webworms and other insects.
54. Listen to the radio or television for information.
55. Evaluate your widgets.
56. Avoid dangling jewelry, drawstrings, anything that might get caught in the machinery.
57. Search for clues in your past.
58. Distribute accountabilities.
59. Do penance and purify your conscience by a good confession.
60. Design your code for simplicity and reliability.
61. Inject approximately 1/2 ml of Depomedrol® as deep as you can between the skin and the cartilage of the ear canal.
62. Determine whether functional requirements can be met by the functionality delivered.
63. Develop a strong feeling of cherishing each and every living being.
64. Remember to breathe.
65. Use slip-resistant flooring. Falling with a hot casserole or a sharp knife in your hand can have serious consequences.
66. Do not listen to naysayers, naggers or depressed people.
67. Be aware of streams, drainage channels and other areas known to flood suddenly.
68. Meet as many news directors as you can.
69. Purge your possessions.
70. Caulk and weatherstrip around doors and windows to plug air leaks.
71. Use your free hand to stretch your skin.
72. Acknowledge epiphanies.
73. Clean and disinfect everything.
74. Find a mentor who will challenge you.
75. Collaborate with outside partners.
76. Use body language to show interest.
77. Talk slowly in a soothing voice (it doesn't have to be monotone).

78. Stop being concerned what the rest of the world says about you.
79. Change the water in bird baths at least once a week or install a fountain or dripper to keep the water moving.
80. Realize your true self in the pool of wisdom.
81. Declare your love, very publicly.
82. Secure your home and relocate animals to a safe place on higher ground.
83. Do not underestimate spiritual opposition.
84. Think about sex in a new way.
85. Avoid television or any other distraction that may dampen your spiritual focus.
86. Buy two sets of appropriate gym wear.
87. Drill a hole into the skull to increase the volume of blood in the brain.
88. Have your home tested for radon.
89. Get in touch with your pain and emotions.
90. Remember that not getting what you want is sometimes a wonderful stroke of luck.
91. Always clean up messes and spills and store food in airtight containers.
92. Never dump anything down a storm drain.
93. Use a point of contact for the release of your faith.
94. Keep your body covered as much as possible.
95. Prepare answers to common questions.
96. Try to do things with your non-dominant hand.
97. Expect the Spirit to move upon your vocal organs and to put supernatural words on your lips.
98. If you check into a hotel room and something is conspicuously damaged or missing, take a picture immediately.
99. Build a miniature model.
100. Get in the habit of stopping to ask, "What is on my mind right now?"
101. Avoid slow-burning, smouldering fires.
102. Call your City Council and attend the next meeting.

103. Listen to the right types of music.
104. Find the best time to do repetitive and boring tasks.
105. Read a book of poetry.
106. Revegetate or mulch disturbed soil as soon as possible.
107. Prepare for disasters.
108. Snap a picture of important people you meet, and add that photo to your contacts.
109. Leave little love notes everywhere.
110. Consider getting dressed up for your interview, even though no one will see you.
111. Make sure what you want is available.
112. Accept that you may need to make a few adjustments.
113. If you are going to pray aloud, pray in tongues. Otherwise, pray to yourself quietly.
114. Think about your research as you fall asleep.
115. Stick your tongue straight out of your mouth, trying to keep it flat and relaxed.
116. Experience your desire.
117. Repeat the process.

SIX EPISTLES

To Capt. Ganzfeld
c/o Glidding Meadows Airport

Dear Captain Ganzfeld,
    I'm a big fan of yours. I can't believe the way your guffling plumes have inflected our airways. There are messages flatulated by each froompy jet you pass in—the sound means the same as the vapour trail interpreted. My mother says it's coincidence. At first I wasn't that interested. Anyone can scar the skyflesh in a Messerschmitt or Spitfire, and just because the jets become supersonic at times doesn't mean they're less of a nuisance. But that nuisance, I began to realize as I developed into a girl (what I was before, they won't tell me), was becoming a *new sense* of possibility. Your gorgeous jets quickly became my reason for living, superseding hippopotami (too long to explain). While you were up there concocting aerial soufflés, I was down here on the roof of the greenhouse scratching away because of an unremitting skin condition. They actually put one of those dog cones on my head so I couldn't claw the sides of my face too easily. What shitty embarrassment! But the upside of it was that your cumuloid arias were even more pronounced and better articulated to my ear than they had been before the imposition of the cone. Yes, I was scratching away quite heartily when it occurred to me that you could be getting a much wider audience for your work. Since that time, I have been controlling you telepathically. Nothing too extreme, mostly just the repetition of certain ravishing patterns and blossoming frumpages.
    Now, I'm not an educated person: my aunt on my father's side speaks every fourth word and my uncle on my mother's side speaks every word all the time, and it's sadly been damaging to him. Great clumps of verbiage he can't help spewing out. His mouth is broken now and he's unable to keep anything in. Before

the onset of his concrescent logorrhoea, he was a wizard among dermatologists, and I'm sure he's my only hope of restitution. I have long pleaded for his help and he now says, by semaphore, that he'll cure me if you'll cut out that racket. He's quite willing to go fist to fist with you, but I tell him you're not that kind of man. I even tell him you're not that kind, and that you're not of man. Still, he wants to at least go sword to toe with you. All he does is watch television all day. He claims it energizes him and nourishes his lunar plexus. Now personally I think you could take him. But supposing you succeed—there'll be no one to remove my affliction. On the other hand, if you fail and he kills you, well, we've lost one of the great artists of our age. Here's my solution: you stay up there in your dainty black jets and then, while he levitates during a commercial break, I will let the air out of him. He'll become a sheet I can fold and lay as a healing blanket across my blotches. If all of this sounds a bit convoluted, I apologize. I just wanted you to know how deeply I admire what you do and when you do it, but that you may be in just a bit of trouble because of the foregoing implication. If at any time you want the spell broken—my remote control spell, I mean—just say these words and you'll plummet like a nest of goslings worn as a hat by a woman who's just been struck by a bail of hay. I know, you're probably wishing by now that you'd never heard from me. I thought it important, however, that you realize your actions are largely due to impulses of my imagination. It is only because I care very deeply for you, and because I have ivy growing on my leg cast, that I am confessing these things. It will not explain the lizards in your bathwater—they're largely metaphorical, I suspect—but it will give you some insight into why you've flown over my urban farm seven times in the last hour alone. My mother thinks it's because of a neurological condition. Do I flatter myself too much to dream that it might be something more? Something outside of either my control or yours? Love is a neurological condition, isn't it? It grows on the sides of buildings and they chop it down with hoes. But our love, I fantasize, would be different. Your frowzy

manoeuvring will eat through my disease and the flowers planted there will blossom in your image. I cannot say more without kissing this photo of your fuselage (I crouched in the copse with a telephoto lens one afternoon). I cannot betray you, but it looks as though—despite my scheme—a duel of some sort may be inevitable now. I'm getting tired of writing this wretched letter to you. I can't even remember what the point of it was now. Also, cracks have begun to form in the ceiling, and it sounds like there are ungodly things giving birth up there. Please make your jets go sweetly, and kick up a little extra rumpy flamboyance on this next pass. We'll never bring our ancestors back from the dead unless you roar like the prince of swords I know you are. There's no simple answer. Everything has its consequences. I guess I'll just sleep on it. No one else is. And when I close my eyes a dog barks. So there you have it: we've come full circle, and beyond that it's all cheap photographs and dried-up froth.
    Lasciviously,
    Velocity

~

Stuart Ross
Chief Groomer
Proper Tails Pet Salon

Dear Mr. Ross,
    The poems you ordered have at last arrived at our warehouse and will be shipped immediately pending your approval. We think you will find these pieces—in the "surrealistic" genre—to be well-crafted and of a generally high calibre.
    Regrettably, however, one of the poems sustained some slight damage during transportation from our factory in Thedford to our warehouse in West Toronto. The poem in question is the one we ourselves had recommended in response to your interest in "something anecdotal with a high verb count, not too dirty"—the

pastoral-flavoured "Frickitt's Curve" (Item #10485). Only two short segments have been affected, and not necessarily, I might venture, for the worse. The phrase intended to read "amber-gloved clothesline pole erectors" now reads "taffy-coloured birdbath inspectors," and the line ending "hose down the tracks at railway stops" now ends "hoe down the racks at tailor shops." While we believe these flaws to have resulted from careless handling during transit, we're investigating the possibility that the employee who produced this piece failed to abide by our plant's strict specifications regarding the proper application of semantic fixative. As none of the other poems suffered similar alterations, we cannot rule out this theory.

Having already kept you waiting longer than we should have liked, it will be our pleasure to ship these items free of charge the moment you give us the go-ahead. In addition, we will happily include an additional instalment of the modular poem "The Turbulated Curtain," as we know from past orders this title is among your favourites manufactured by our company.

On behalf of all of us at TVI, please accept my apology for this incident and know that in future we will do everything in our power to promptly meet your poetry needs. We thank you for your patience and understanding as we eagerly await your reply.

Yours Sincerely,
Virgil Troop
Chief Executive Supervisor of Customer Service
Department of Poetry and Other Engineered Texts
Torpor Vigil Industries
Toronto, Ontario

~

To Mr. Khropft and Mr. Polymer
of the Kilchrist Larval Ointment Co.

Gentlemen, I have attained a new glow, and I am convinced it is attributable solely to your tonics. I thank you with all my life and wish the same horrid blessing upon you each.

    Yours Lustrously,
    Lord Clack

PS: I can't believe my garments alone are making so much noise!

~

Madam Quince-Dowry
Where She Lives

Dear Madam Quince-Dowry,
    As summer is ending I felt it incumbent on me to invite you to a thunderstorm which is scheduled to take place outside the herring factory this evening at dusk. You needn't dress in any but the most perfunctory manner nor bring any crickets (there will be plenty of those!) as I myself will be wearing but a thin military camisole from the pelvic region upwards and will be toting a gecko or two. By the way, I can see the dunes from the third-storey window of my cabin, and they are absolutely still—not a grain moving—at this time of day. I know not what lies within them, but I have a friend (a recent lover of yours, say the boys down at the pub) who is a spelunker and *he* says he's not interested in them because they're not caves. I've asked him not to accompany us and he's more than happy to oblige. Will there be fireworks? No, there will not be fireworks, but there's a young Christian girl (a bastard daughter of yours, if the Reverend Glitch is to be believed) who will read from the Bible for tips and cheese. I'm so excited by the prospect that you might actually join me on this little outing that I've quite been masturbating—and furiously!—all morning in anticipation. Dr. Craque (the same fellow who, according to the papers, performed your last hysterectomy) told me this would be good for calming my nerves—indeed the opposite, for I find myself in a quasimanic frenzy just contemplating the notion that you and I might picnic together this very

evening beneath those same bolts of lightning which are sure to set the Riddley barns aflame again. Have you any toothpaste? Be sure to screw the cap on tightly: I have an aunt (one of your mothers, I believe?) who died not long ago from leaving the cap unscrewed on a tube of Sterident. The poor woman left the world without a will, and we've been squabbling over her miniature teacups ever since. Please respond by flare (red yes, blue no) as soon as possible. I must close now as my wife (your squirrel-catcher in a past life, swears Sturluson the trance medium and elbow boxer) is leaving on her errands and I would like for her to deliver this letter, along with the rooster I borrowed, to your hallowed door.

    With Fondest Regards to you and your lovely poodle (does she suffer yet?),
    Your Dithering Suitor,
    Andromimicus "Andy" Clump, Esq.

~

The Discrete Acquisitions & Deployment Co.
Night Wind Dept.,
Attn.: L. Rug
Wollongong, Australia

Dear Lester Rug or Similar,
    The wombats arrived safely, each in its own decorative encasement. Problem is, I can't tell them apart, they're all so cheerful. Is this typical, or is it just me? Are they indeed separate entities, one from another, or simply biological aliases of one source-wombat? Please get back to me at your leisure as the situation is not urgent and we're likely to be all dead—I mean, to all be dead!—by the time a communication does arrive. Best of luck with your new position (hope the department lets you keep those "documents").
    Hopelessly,
    Mogby Rumpidge
    Kelpwich Investments

For Prompt Delivery
To Col. Q. V. Wive
of the Beyond

Dear Colonel Wive,

My hairdresser has advised me that it would be prudent and auspicious for me to leave the world at this time. Trusting to your good counsel, which served me so well during my short apprenticeship with you at the Wayfarers' Academy prior to your own death, I felt loath to make any plans regarding this matter without seeking your opinion.

I fully appreciate that there are limitations placed upon you by the state of non-being vis-à-vis communication with those such as myself who are, albeit provisionally, among the so-called living; nonetheless, I am bold and selfish enough to hope that you might be able to reply for old times' sake with a simple yea or nay, should even that not prove too difficult or inconvenient.

I know that this will not enhance the probability of a swift response, but I must confess that I never liked you. In fact, to be perfectly honest, I disliked you. I'll be the first to confirm that we had some wonderful times together and that, in all our mediocre yet transcendent dealings, never once did you treat me in a manner that could be called anything but decent, cordial and fair. It was just something about you, I guess, and I'm sure it couldn't have been helped. And yet this little revulsion of mine hasn't stopped me, after all these comfortable years, from approaching you for a favour at a time of great personal importance.

I will cut to the chase. What I need desperately to know (to paraphrase the bard) is (to do it again) this: should I or should I not snuff it?

Now, I don't want to pressure you too much—after all, you are dead—but if you could see fit to get back to me within four business days, that would be most congenial to my present spiritual and financial situation. Never mind why—I know you never cared much for details. Just answer me, please, to the fullest extent you are capable within—do I ask too much?—the specified time frame (an interval which is, my lawyer agrees, quite reasonable).

Thank you in advance for your fiercely conscientious attention to the subject disclosed above by your ardent ex-student and disinclined admirer,

Zeddy Thraft, BA

PS: A rat that appeared to bear your features just scampered past my feet as I finished jotting this. Seemed odd—thought I'd mention.

FRICKITT'S CURVE

Ginger bashed the cupcakes off the pedestal and Wilmer dragged down the dusty daffodils with his jumbo skewing rod while Catherine elbowed blackbirds off the checkerboard without being too particular about it. Ravagers, in the meanwhile, pillaged the greengrocer's in the guise of pharmaceutical surveyors brandishing scatalogical catapults that we called "glough swinches." No one other than Keith injured any of the large goldfish or followed his instincts too far. Under the old guard we used to postpone cautioning the flimps (I forget what they are) for hours. Anyone who was anyone came out of the woodwork and shed a tear or tore a shed. Manfreda could always be counted on for ingesting the worst brand of manure, so much so that we arranged our appointments around her. Taffy-coloured bird bath inspectors came and went. Molasses salesmen slithered through the pantry while wetting their trousers and mumbling to the dead. Jackie-Sue's daughter's teacher's dog killer stalked through the fruit cellar swinging a map turtle on a string, all the while pretending he was back at the office curtailing his secretary. Vagrants by the dozen, their sockets blazing, waddled past the scullery window shouting hymn snippets and prices. Anyone who wasn't nailed down seemed to transvene upon us in those days. But that was before Harvey started squishing mushrooms through keyholes, and Karen and Melissa started vaselining the retrievers and other short-haired dogs or even dotty spinsters and anybody else who wished to suffer from such slickness. Even church meetings took on a spiritual hue when Rev. Bringiton began jumping and couldn't stop. Kettie nearly died from laughter and Blain resumed twisting breasts and goiters and whatever else he could find dangling. Precipices lost their meaning. What once was tangled became stretched to such an extent we had to commercialize the riverbeds and hoe down the racks at tailor shops. Great bludgeons occurred, tendrils of exploding moss suffocated us from head to toe, but otherwise everything was more or less normal. Screaming faces plastered themselves to the windows of passing trains in verisimilitudes of horror and perhaps alimentary discomfort. Wanda started shooting cats (though I suppose it was in the family). Carlyle ended up in the asylum (but then I guess he was getting paid). And the elderly, come to think of it, began passing away, one by one, in a strange conspiracy of transmigration, leaving us to tend this clumsy world with our own devices.

BEAUTIFUL THOUGHTS

Clear
your mind

of all thoughts

except
the ones

you are currently

thinking

•

There is
nothing

you can't
become

so
don't even bother

not becoming

everything

We've got
enough bombs
to blow up
the world
a hundred times

and yet

we don't
have the guts
to do it

•

Always be kind
to strangers

you never know
when you might meet
the Buddha
in disguise

or some
asshole
who's going
to report
you

There is
a universe

in which
I iron

the same
pair of pants

over and over again

forever

•

Your poverty
is God's way
of punishing
you

for not making

enough
money

The
good news

is that
the government
has fallen

the bad news

is that it
has fallen
on us

•

She refused
to buy

baby oil

because
she thought
it was

inhumane

The least
you can do

is be
magnificent

•

Mommy

said
the awed
little girl

*I want to climb up
every drainpipe
in the world*

It comes
screaming down
the centuries
to greet us

and we're never
home

when
it arrives

•

I have
such wonderful
memories
of our time
together

if only
I could

remember them

One needs one's
higher faculties

to determine

whatever it is
one is doing

down there

on the floor

•

It has now
been

over seven hours

since I began

writing this
sentence

If you can
hear these words

outside of
your head

call the number

on the back
of your radio

•

Let's see—
shall I be
Decadent
or Primitive...?
Decadent or
Primitive...?

Tonight
she is
sad

she is

all over

the world

•

Most things

don't happen

The meek
shall inherit
the earth

though
there may not
be much
left of it

after
the bold

have had
their day

•

Nature
has gone
wild

we're going
to have to
teach it

a lesson

One word
is not enough

to say that

one word
is enough

•

Wholesome Goodness™

from the people

who'd rather
see you

dead

Art is long

Life is short

therefore

you should
invest in art

while
you're still

alive

•

I'm sorry—
there's been
a mistake:

those *weren't*
the days

after all

AFTERNOON OF THE NEEDLE GNOMES

Stealing softly and sharply into a spinster's trance, they come. Soaked in sunbeams of the cataleptic day, gleaming, these tiny slender men, if men they be, jumble forthright onto the white shag carpet of the living room where no flop-eared terrier dares intervene. They have her, the lonely old lady, immobilized by some alien spell. "We've come for burnt meat," they squeak in unison; and then, telepathically: "But we like tarts too."

What she wants to say is "Let me fix you a little something," but no words emerge, and she wonders anyway if her choice of words, had they been heard, might not have offended. But they *are* little, and their long pins glint like tinsel.

Why is everything so unusual today? Why is my body torpid but my senses in vigil? The jays have stopped calling. There are no children at play. No neighbours return with trunks full of groceries, echoing their doorslams against bay-windowed bungalows. What is it, that my thoughts are so clear but my body so slow, while these men like hummingbirds jab and giggle then are stern again?

A jet roars, scorching and sudden, over the neighbourhood. The little men disperse in a twinkling, leaving her to ponder, now mobile, a spill of needles on the carpet at her feet, a dog in want of comforting, and the memory of visitors mysterious yet not unpleasant, of a make and manner rarely seen in her part of town. Perhaps they'll come again when she's better disposed to host them. That would be nice.

THE TIN OF FANCY EXCREMENTS:
A JOURNEY OF THE SELF

Chapter One
The Industrial Powder Rooms

The greyness of the city, in cold steam, draws us back to its industrial powder rooms with their blue skeletons and pneumatic tweezers, their gold-mirrored walls and coiled tubes. I thought they'd boarded up these places years ago, but we simply wandered in, unobstructed, through a doorway in the drainage tunnel behind the mall. The dust hasn't even settled onto the abattoir-like red marble countertops and Victorian dental chairs. The floors, still stained here and there with blood, are tiled in hyperrealist staircase motifs—a cruel deception for tormented souls with no path of escape. The ceilings, with their pressed-tin evil eyes, however, draw your gaze upward into a mesmeric grid of illusory surveillance.

I don't even know much about these spaces except that they were preliminary to some kind of sacrificial performance or display and that their purpose involved cosmetic grooming. Why were so many of them required? Windowless and interconnected, these dolorous yet pristine urban catacombs serve to remind us that we know very little about even our most recent ancestors; that one generation can preserve secrets from its immediate successors; and that the value of personal hygiene and grooming—even if administered by violent strangers—is supreme in any era.

Chapter Two
The Burial

Striking off on my own, and changing tenses, I climbed a long narrow staircase. After exploring for some time the doorless hallway at the top, I came to a row of soft brown featureless mammals, all hanging this way and that on the grey putty-veneered wall. Further along the purple hardwood floor, the ceiling was open to the stars, ceasing thus to be a ceiling at all.

Here I became aware of an antique odour rising, through time and space, from the tin of excrement I'd buried the week before in defiance of my beloved's wishes. I'd been outside the gates of the occult dairy. Whether I'd gone there expressly for the interment or was merely taken by the whim as I passed, I cannot recall. The tin had been in my wife's family for years. It was granted my possession only on the condition that I return it after walking a distance sufficient to satisfy my urge. But as soon as I got the thing I was off, like a cat with a morsel of roasted turkey dropped on the linoleum by a doddering arthritic oaf.

The burial took no more than half an hour and was watched by a lachrymose police officer whose behaviour was consistent with someone suffering from seasonal affective disorder, inoperable barometric distress syndrome and acute male menopause. Priests from the dairy did not bother me. And suddenly the air was filled with ochre fluff. Descending and ascending, it seemed to propel me into a state of imperial contentment, as if the gods were telling me that life is pointless but I should be happy anyway and, for what it matters, I'd done the right thing.

But how could I return home empty-handed to the tungsten and lint and cat dander of my in-laws' apartment and explain all this to the woman who'd loved me moderately for years despite my abiding desultory air and bouts of involuntary ventriloquy? She would not understand—I would simply have to flee and not look back.

That is how I came to find myself, a week later, strutting rancorously upon the recently polished floorboards of a roofless passageway leading ever on towards a mystery I didn't even care about. My aimless pilgrimage had led me, against all odds, to a place without ledges where nothing fell from the sky. I crushed a beetle in a nutcracker and wept for my sins.

Chapter Three
A Little Show

*At 6:02 a.m. a Little Show will commence
beneath the Commodious and Redoubtable Skirts of
Larissa the Superfluous
complete with Aztec Mermaids, Hypnotized Elizabethan Emus,
Turkish Mathematicians doing Impossible Sums,
Recumbent Houseboat Contractors &
Tom the Clairvoyant Weimaraner
~ Children & Elderly welcome ~*

I stared scornfully yet wistfully at the broadside and tried to scrape it off the glass of the inset firehose case with my fingernails, but it hung all the more tenaciously there—for who to see? The grey putty wall had ended jaggedly just as the passageway looked like it would become too narrow to get through. I turned around to see a middle-aged man and woman, nude except for bowling shoes and vertically striped knee socks, running towards me down the hall, waving machetes. They looked possessed by ancient and malignant spirits, saliva overflowing their lower lips. It hardly seems sensible but I waited for them to catch up with me. Their machetes carved the air ever more menacingly as they uttered quiet guttural barks. Finally, almost out of breath, they reached the spot where I stood staring in bewilderment.

My carelessness in not attempting to elude them must have spoiled their plan. They slumped, panting dreadfully, with hands on knees, the knives still in their grip but visibly aquiver. I put a hand on the gentleman's shoulder, for he seemed to be in worse shape. Then I retracted it and wiped the sweat onto the behind of my trousers, reviled as I always am by any bodily liquids, gases or solids issuing from another man's body. And the woman, I daren't touch, lest there appear to be prurient intent behind my action.

It was some time before they caught their breath—and I mean a very long time. My initial compassion and concern turned to boredom then consternation. Eventually they spoke, gasping and gulping as they shared the monologue:

"We may have scared you...not a little. It's...the first time we've...done it. We're...we're sweating and salivating...so much we're...getting a chill. We use Dr. Krittaways'...Spittle Pills. We're working...on a grant...from the National...Arts Foundation. We weren't intending...to actually kill...anyone. We're pleased...to meet you."

And they extended sweaty trembling hands, which I reluctantly clasped. Names were exchanged and the woman sank to her knees while the man slouched against what remained of the wall. I looked at my watch and shrugged. An announcement came over the loudspeaker system but I couldn't catch a word of it—so garbled and mean and distorted it made my face twitch.

As they were themselves artists of some sort, I decided to share with them my visionary idea for civic improvement.

Chapter Four
My Idea

What I conceive of, basically, is a monument to my beloved's most ravishing blouse. To be made of burnished bronze, this extraordinary sculpture will stand approximately three storeys high in the middle of our busiest intersection. It's an idea that came to me through my higher self, guided by the ascended masters of the Far East, so please don't call it sexist. There was an exalted, numinous quality to that blouse and I'd like to see its transformative powers radiate through our fair but unenlightened city. Also, it will give me occasion to remember her form as I drive past each morning on my way to the cannery, but that's not the main reason I want it built. All that stands in the way now is the funding, and the fact that the Hopi prophecies seem to be coming true at an alarming rate. So please help us build the ravishing blouse monument before the end of the world. We're counting on your support.

Chapter Five
On a Mission!

Only a few minutes had it taken me to outline my proposal, yet I found upon concluding that my two new friends had fallen fast asleep, so exhausted were they by their artistic activities. At that moment, or just a moment later, my cellphone rang. It wasn't my beloved calling to say that she missed me and that she didn't give a damn about the excrement, that I should just come home where I belong. No, it was someone from the Civic Iotas and Scintillas Department phoning to inform me that my lost uncle Tim-Phillipe—or, as we call him, Glen—had been found and that I should go to such and such an address immediately. It turns out the address was for a sluice spigot factory a few blocks away.

Upon arrival, I spoke with the foreman, a white woman, who said they'd found Glen that morning wandering through the smelting hangar with his mouth dangling open, catching sunlight. Forsaking speech, he'd attempted to communicate by dipping his fingers in a pouch of damp blue chalk and rubbing them on the skin of a tangerine. And the odd thing is, they claim to have understood him perfectly. It seems he fancies himself a highly intelligent botanical life form that just happens to resemble humans, or maybe he said it was mimicry. In any case, his expressed goal is to obtain a position as a social contractor while studying the effects of being gradually eaten alive by a vegetarian lynx he plans to keep in a closet. To this end he sought the help of those at the factory who were willing to hear of his ambition. While this was being related to me, two of the smelters wheeled him towards us on a dolly. And now, striking a fern-like pose, my uncle stood before me.

How I had the wherewithal to do what I did next, I've no idea. I took from my vest pocket a perforating disc, like a finely spiked pizza-cutter, and ran it lightly across my uncle's left cheek. The effect was instantaneous and imperceptible. We stood almost motionless for several seconds, waiting. The drone of the machinery was beginning to loosen my muscles. At the same time, the seams of my vest and shirt were starting to rapidly unstitch, as were the seams of my trousers (my boxer shorts were at the dry cleaners). I slunk to the iron floor as my clothes fell from my body.

The reconnaissance mission was turning into a complete failure, but I didn't care. I felt that a forbidden freedom denied me since early childhood, infancy perhaps, was suddenly mine again. I didn't understand a word that was being said so far above me. An antediluvian sigh shuffled from my lips as I curled and coiled and wriggled in a foolish endocrinilogical pudding of objectless sensuality. Warm pee (my own, of course) flooded across my belly. All sounds were muffled as they wove together into synaesthesic orgone blankets, enveloping me in pure endorphinous comfort. Good God, was I ever relaxed! I began to laugh quietly, a whimpering blissful laugh. I knew that this was the moment I'd been waiting for all my life, and it was upon me so suddenly. But then, where did it go?

The next thing I knew, I was in semi-darkness on a cold metal floor, anxious and alone. Light from a streetlamp seeped in through oily yellow window panes, cracked by years of mediating the industrial world and nature. My ears were ringing but the vast room was silent. What remained of my clothes had been draped over me, a sweat-soaked rug barely hiding my nakedness. I shivered in a nauseous chill, teeth chattering. Tears ran from my right eye down to my left eye then on, with the others (those originating in the left eye), to the floor. I could smell oil and rotting wood, and that was my only solace. Yet I felt strangely purified. I resolved to embrace my miserable condition and move forward into new and potentially providential states. Something marvellous was awaiting, I could feel it! Then I changed my mind and flopped back into my dreary cold malaise, confident I'd never get off the floor of the factory and never find my way out even if I did. I spent a long wretched night in foetal position, interrupted at times by spans of elegant delirium.

Chapter Six
A Jealous Dream

I awoke without a sound and fell over a hot cliff into a clutter of quasi-ecumenical transhuman clay, some of which was alive. Bruised, winded, scuffed, still thick with aftersleep, I watched a flock of shabby blimps trawling for skydivers and hang-gliders in a slippery turquoise sky splattered with cloudlets. There was something unswallowable about this day, something that stuck in my craw that I couldn't quite wrap my head around or put my finger on. Maybe it was the sound of those goddamned electronic church bells, wobbling towards me like a belligerent gang of flatulent basset hounds. Maybe it was the smell of cooked sewage emanating from somewhere within the gated community just beyond the claypatch. Or maybe it was just the dream I'd had. Yes—the dream. I think it was the dream....

I'd dreamt that my cherished beloved, whom I'd abandoned so impetuously, was living in a farmhouse with washed-up race-car drivers who were competing for sexual conquest of the sole female resident. This was the premise of the reality TV show being filmed by a lecherous crew of chauvinist techies bent on capturing every sanctified moment of my innocent darling's existence. Having seen part of the first episode on a high-definition wide-screen television set at O'Blurmny's Pub, where I'd gone to play laser crokinole, I flew to the rescue. But upon arriving at the farm, I found myself restricted from approaching close enough to call out to her. Physically restrained, I could do nothing but watch in jealous anguish (and of course concern for her dignity) as my precious spouse prepared to take her turn in the outdoor bathtub, beneath the pornographic gaze of dozens of macho onlookers and, ultimately, millions of television viewers.

It was at that point that I vomited myself awake and tumbled from the back of the city-bound vegetable truck onto the wet gravel of a country lane. Some stars were still visible as the morning fog drew across the sky, allowing the night to change discreetly into day.

Chapter Seven
Something Pleasant

By mid-afternoon—having groped my way through an increasingly familiar landscape—I reached the outskirts of the communal settlement where I'd once worked as a junior threat detector and eco-semiologist. I knew I could get some clothes there and a bite to eat, and it would be an ideal place for yet another change of tense.

I'm soon greeted by the paramilitary neo-hippie security squad, who welcome me with open arms of both types (fortunately they miss with both). After leading me into camp, they give me a perfectly ripe avocado and a pair of standard-issue violet and taupe overalls. I check into one of the canvas enclosures that serve as living quarters for guests.

It's implausibly dark in my tent, even with the curtains torn off and worn as kilts by the marauding mandrills, their outlandishly sexy asses—what was God thinking!—covered at last. At least the dimness makes it easier to nap, so I do, but not for long because I want to be on my way again before nightfall.

Leaving the tent, I stroll towards the hillside stairway I used to climb now and again during my sojourn at the camp, when I was off duty. I happen to be joined by a charming young woman I've never met—likely one of the new breed of geolinguists who travel from settlement to settlement. Clouds break and the afternoon gloominess gives way to sudden brilliance.

As we ascend the hillside stair of old tongues, pelts and feathers, I say, "I always like going up here, because there's always something pleasant on the other side."

She smiles wanly, then, when she thinks I'm not looking, curls her upper lip and rolls her eyes in a kind of okay-mister-if-you-say-so expression—no doubt recalling the corporeal atrocities she's seen just over the hill on other excursions.

Right, I remember. *It's never pleasant at all—must be just a "mask memory" hiding the grisly impressions scarred into my brain on previous ascents.*

We rise a few steps more.

"You know," I say. "I just remembered there's a baby meadow vole that needs to be bottle-fed back at the encampment. Maybe I should..."

She nods and smiles, like a mother who's just caught her youngest tax consultant's pet owl in a leg trap.

Back down in the valley, I see a shimmering geodesic dome that wasn't there when I left for the stairs. Its gossamer skin ripples in the breeze. As I near, I see that this covering appears to have been made by spiders—large, fast spiders. The web is so intricate and light as to dazzle all retinal and rational expectations. I get too close and breathe a hole in it, then the damn thing collapses, quilliferous lattice and all.

I'm not having much luck today. Maybe I should head into town.

Chapter Eight
In a Strange Town

After a quick smoked pickerel sandwich (which happens to be outstanding), I leave the settlement on foot and amble down into a meandering ravine that leads, in my memory, to a monorail station at the perimeter of the city. But the deeper I wander into this lush slash across the landscape, the more religiously, existentially and (worst of all) physically lost I become. A butterfly lands on my forearm and bites me fiercely until I bleed. I'm too squeamish about guts to squash it, but I certainly didn't expect the brutish laceration it inflicts. Nor did I expect the sight that lies beyond the next curve of the ravine—though I could swear I saw it once in a dream.

Spread out before me is a town of modest size sitting in a valley scooped out at the terminus of the ravine. It seems typical of many other villages I've seen that date from the late 1800s, except for one thing—or rather many things, all of which are water towers. Why would one small town need so many elevated water storage structures? The question hardly crosses my mind, for I am swept away by their benign and lofty majesty as they loom imperiously over the churches and factories, the houses, schools and shops of the town. It is as if all the water towers of the world have been assembled to astound me. I descend the verdant slope of mown grass to walk among this forest of architectural marvels, each tower distinct: here a futuristic ovoid steel column, there a modernist brick obelisk, in the distance a classical concrete pillar. A brooding gothic megalith might neighbour a sleek minimalist spindle. An imposing archaeo-industrial needle might stand aflank a neo-romantic ivory tower.

There are people in this town, but always in the distance. No one is ever close enough for me to ask the name of the place, and any sign I see—though they all appear to be in English—is curiously incomprehensible, as though the misplacement of a single letter here or there has rendered the whole of its typography illegible.

So I wander in this strange town, alone in my serene astonishment, down empty streets of eroding asphalt painted with the shadows of monolithic wonders.

In a cul-de-sac at the end of a placid residential street, as eerily deserted as the others, stands an elegant cylinder of pre-stressed concrete that fans outward towards its top, twenty or so metres in the air. There are vertically elongated windows of lapis blue glass high up on its shaft. On either side of it extends a tall hedge obscuring the view beyond.

A small dog—a dwarf Appalachian terrier, I think—dashes onto the road and rolls onto its back at my feet, wanting to be petted. I scruffle it behind the ears and tickle its tummy before resuming my approach to the tower. The pup seems satisfied and does not follow.

At the cream-coloured tower's base is an archway the size of a door. The salty smell of the sea greets me as I enter the tunnel. In the short time it takes me to reach the far opening, twilight has fallen. The clouds, in striated mounds, are purple and orange above the sea.

With the mysterious town at my back, I walk across the sand until, about a half-kilometre along its granular expanse, I arrive at a vacant beach gazebo with the number 3 painted in violet pink on its roof. This day, like all others, has been long. It's time for another of my naps. And where better to nap than in the cozy seaside confines of Gazebo No. 3?

Chapter Nine
The Night Picnic

It's nighttime and there is a sickening volley of *glorps* emanating from the soggy sands beside the pier, where wet delinquents pirouette into the frothy drink. There must be something horrid over there on the drenched beach—something the fuzzy glow of flying saucers has failed to illuminate. It is, perhaps, the sound of some invisible nastiness, such as a sasquatchean ghost plucking giant crabs from their saturated embedments. I can think of nothing else that could make such a harrowing nocturnal concerto.

Let us turn our thoughts away from this unsolvable mystery that so perturbs me, if it's all the same to you, and cast our perceptual net across the other length of the strand, where fiercely cheerful picnics have broken out at the foot of grand mammarian dunes lit by the arabesque flight paths of fireflies drunk with summer lust. There, beneath torches shaded in gloxinia blue and canopies striped in persimmon and aubergine, our revellers dine on fresh-caught shellfish barbecued over hallucinogenic embers. It seems that nothing could disturb the easy humour of these rakishly hairy men and brashly sensuous women, celebrating life together beneath the approving constellations that glitter to match each twinkle in their jovial Atlantean eyes. What a welcome sight this is to you who have just begun your travels on this night and I who have been wandering for days.

As this scene grows closer with each footfall, our hearts soar to match the good spirits of our neighbours, into whose company we will soon be welcomed as fellow lovers of life.

But wait! They've spotted us and are charging this way with their fish-gutting knives and oyster shuckers! Quick—onto that abandoned speedboat! Oh, damn, the motor won't start! Dear God, there must be something to throw, or something to— There! The gasoline! Grab that can of... *Huh?* They're laughing at us? They've stopped just short of massacring us and are having a damn good laugh at our expense. Very funny. Ha-ha-ha. That's it—wipe the tears away and go back to your bloody picnic, you twisted bastards. Yeah, that's it—moon us, you creepy broads. God, you'd think I would have learned by now. I guess I was bound to fall for it sooner or later. Do I ever need a tranquillizer. Well, enough of this. No more roaming among the psychos for me. I'm going home.

Chapter Ten
Back Home at Last, I Await the New Age

Leeches on damp trees, spongiferous clouds clotting the horizon, a tube of eye shadow dropped from the purse of a hang-gliding transvestite executive, a spider's web shimmering between a nude woman's sleeping corgis: these are the things of which the dawn is made (along with bashed letters, a gilded furnace pipe and three milking dollies lying aslant in the tousled ditches alongside Highway 402 about three kilometres west of the turnoff to Watford.)

All this splendour—a veritable pornutopia of overlooked objects ready to be found and labelled by some fresh goal-oriented mind—and I can't seem to find my way out of bed. A compass and an icepick would be useful, I'm sure, as would 130 milligrams of pure caffeine in the form of boiled potable water poured over a tablespoon of ground and filtered pre-roasted coffee beans—now, why is that illegal!—but all I have is this pen and paper, and, as every schoolchild who read *A Colloquy of Grievances* knows, I couldn't write myself out of a wet paper bag let alone a bed of this strength and vastness. There must be a way to bring the world to me—some kind of inner net that could be projected outward to encircle the globe, capturing even the least predictable objects: flashing horse brassieres, cellphone toupées, electric face slappers and more—much, much more. Voracious engines could search for whatever I desire, load it onto the net and send it hurtling towards me at furious speed, only for it to stop an instant before impact, right at my fingertips. Such technology may still be several months away, but I'm willing to wait. I will be in this bed, according to my latest calculations, until the Thirteenth Baktun dwindles away and the shadow of the plumed serpent descends the stone steps of Chichen Itza. I will be here until the local garbage bylaws change and free men and women are allowed to throw out whatever they want whenever they want. Prone, I will lie, with my blindfold and comforter and foam-rubber pillow, until the bargains become unbeatable and a new age dawns.

DISTENDED APHORISMS

There's a time and a place for everything, but it's not now and it's certainly not here.

Everybody has to pay the piper, but you might not have to pay him much if he happens to be non-union.

Tomorrow is a new day, but the day after that has been made up of recycled moments you were too busy and depressed to notice.

Intelligence is the ultimate aphrodisiac, but a dab of extract from a civet's anal gland and a nice pair of shoes will usually work just as well.

What goes around comes around, but don't expect to get any of it unless you've already got too much.

Where there's a will there's a way, but where there's no will there's no way you're going to get anything more than a set of commemorative plates and a busted footstool.

Rome wasn't built in a day, but that was before they invented drywall.

The Lord works in strange and mysterious ways, but then so do serial killers and plumbers.

Laughter is the best medicine, but I'll still take the intravenous Demerol® if it's all the same to you.

Some people try to be tall by cutting off the heads of others, but they're usually apprehended within a few hours.

The road to Hell is paved with good intentions, but I never believe those travel brochures.

Poetry is compensation for the miseries we endure, but that doesn't mean I'm going to drop the lawsuit.

To the pessimist the glass is half empty and to the optimist it's half full, but to the paying customer it's a rip-off no matter how you look at it.

A woman's work is never done, but if you do happen to take a break do you think you could grab me a beer?

When the Lord closes a door He opens a window and when He closes a window He opens a door, but if he keeps that up all night I'll have Him evicted.

Time heals all wounds, but if I were you I'd see a doctor just the same.

You have to break a few eggs to make an omelette, but you only have to break one to make a baby.

Life is a tale told by an idiot, full of sound and fury, but death is a short certificate written by a sensible fellow with a degree in forensic pathology.

Pissing in one's shoes will not keep one's feet warm for long, but it's a surefire way to get out of a bad date.

There is no excellent beauty that hath not some strangeness in the proportion, but I'm just saying that to make you feel good.

MANTA RAY JACK AND THE CREW OF THE SPOONER

After climbing the steps of the lighthouse, Shauna was overcome by a wavering queasiness and a quavering wheeziness. Beside her, gazing at the waves, stood the sentry—a veering sniper with the look of a sneering viper.

The focused light in the idle tower shone with the intensity of a locust fight in the tidal hour. In its creeping beam could be seen, far below, a brash hick hawking his wares (a hash brick) while walking his hares, a mock duck and a dairy fox covered in dock muck on the ferry docks, a fawn buyer and a lane mobster at a bonfire eating Maine Lobster™—*"hand-caught and canned hot!"*—and a pretty girl with a Yorkie puppy admiring a gritty pearl with a porky yuppie. Also visible in the roving light was a sprawl of schoonerists whose ship, now docked, was covered in the scrawl of spoonerists.

As she clutched the observation deck's white rail, Shauna spotted something extraordinary and exclaimed, "A right whale!"

"That's not a whale—just a thievious dunderhead," said the sen-

---

MANTA RAY JACK AND THE CREW OF THE SPOONER, ALSO

After climbing the steps of the lighthouse, Shauna was overcome by an oscillating nausea and a trembling asthmatic shortness of breath. Beside her, looking out to sea, stood the sentry—an unsteady sharpshooter with the look of a poisonous snake whose features have been constricted into a contemptible grin.

The source of radiance within the still columnar structure cast its sharply defined beam with all the force of a battle among large swarming grasshoppers at a point in the day when the sea rises or falls due to the gravitational influence of the moon and sun, or perhaps at some cataclysmic juncture in a history not yet known to man or so long past as to be lost from collective awareness. Within its sweeping luminosity could be seen, far below, a mallard decoy and a lactophilic *canid* enslimed on a pier from which a small carrier boat makes its regular voyage to a nearby island and back, a bold rustic lad selling a resinous psychoactive block while exercising his bunnies, a purchaser of young female deer and an alley gangster at a controlled outdoor blaze eating delectable canned crustacean meat from the east coast of the USA, and an attractive young woman holding a baby Yorkshire terrier while observing, in the company of a chubby urban professional, the beauty of a sandy but lustrous accretion yielded up by an oyster. Another thing revealed by the traversing beam was the haphazardly dispersed crew of a schooner at anchor, which appeared to be decorated in the graffiti of punsters or dyslexics.

try, as the starry sky was clouded by a devious thunderhead. He aimed his automatic rifle and fired a rapid volley at the vapid Raleigh (descendant of Sir Walter) splashing haplessly towards shore in his dolphin costume.

Repulsed, Shauna hobbled then whirled as her guts wobbled then hurled.

"Well, he made a piss-poor porpoise, if you ask me," the tall and veering volunteering sentry opined. Then for good measure he shot the foiled sucker daft enough to wave the sail that read SAVE THE WHALE.

Taking a deep breath of the night's charmed air, Shauna retreated into the lighthouse and sank into a comfortably armed chair.

Moments later, the skipper of the schooner ascended and made his entrance, setting on the coffee table the gift of a crude shrew kept for just such an occasion by his shrewd crew. Curiously enough there was a tame sable on the same table.

"We couldn't help but notice that your light was on," announced the captain, "so we thought we'd nop in for a dribble." He went on to explain that he and his sailors, who'd risen in his wake and now

---

Shauna, somewhat recovered, became excited when she looked out over the sea and detected what she thought was a member of a family of cetaceans once almost hunted to extinction. As a mischievous thundercloud obscured the constellated heavens, the sentry (who was, by the way, greater than average in height, swaying somewhat and offering his services free of charge) explained that what she'd spotted was actually just a stupid robber in disguise. Aiming his long-barrelled assault gun, he fired a quick succession of bullets at the figure below—the descendant, in fact, of a venturesome Elizabethan courtier, floundering towards land in a dolphin costume. This vicious display of unwarranted brutality was enough to make poor Shauna lose whatever equilibrium she'd gained and vomit over the ivory guard rail of the observation deck. The sentry's only comment on his horrendous act was that, in his opinion, the victim hadn't made a very convincing marine mammal. Then—merely because he thought him dimwitted, it seems—he also shot the muddied activist who'd been hoisting a banner reading SAVE THE WHALE.

Shauna inhaled a tonic lungful of night air then made her way inside to repose and recuperate in a stuffed piece of furniture designed for comfortable sitting.

At this point, the captain of the docked ship arrived bearing a small furry insectivore as a present, which he set down upon a table that happened to already bear a typically bad-tempered but in this case domesticated mammal of similar features. The captain explained that, seeing the light and presuming someone was home and awake, he and his fellow sailors had decided to "nop in for a dribble"—having intended, no doubt, to say "drop in for a nibble"

75

stood listening intently like a gaggle of capped runts, had been voyaging to Malaysia to enjoy some teriyaki bluefin halibut in a very tacky flu-bin Bali hut notorious for its mystic fillets and fistic melees.

"The perfect place," he noted, "for both a white fish and a fight wish! But," continued the seadog as he began to de-sog from the tiny shower that had befallen his ship as it neared the shiny tower, "on our way to get a Bali tan we were ji-hacked by the Taliban. There we were, you see, minding our biz and binding our mizz when a horde of beard weavers swarmed our decks like a herd of weird beavers."

Then the captain's look turned sheepish and the shrew as it shook turned leapish. "I suppose we weren't *entirely* innocent, as we—after ducking the fog for days—happened to be in the midst of a merry cur hunt. It was off the coast of Afghanistan, where we'd sailed—rigged out like yawl trappers—with a plan to trawl yappers. The crew had been hearing their share about the mutts that lived there: 'If you want to make a killing off sweaters, you should be shearing their hair!'

"Well, the shores overflowed with these fashionable curs, and

---

(unless perhaps the former phrase is seafaring slang meaning "to stop by for a drink" or "to urinate"—though it seems unlikely that a group of sailors would drop anchor and climb to the top of a lighthouse just to relieve themselves). His crew had followed him up the stairs and now listened raptly to his account of their travels, the purpose of which had been to experience the renowned Japanese cuisine of a certain gauche and virulent Balinese shack known as much for its brawling patrons as for its sublime Alaskan fish fillets. The captain, still drying off from a light rainfall, went on to explain that the voyage had been interrupted when they were forcibly boarded by government officials off the coast of Afghanistan (an assertion some geographers might find dubious). He claimed that they were securing their tertiary mast and quietly attending to their own affairs when a squadron of men with profuse and stylish facial hair thronged aboard like a mutant herd of large Canadian rodents.

As if in recollection of the frightening event, the small furry insectivore trembled and began to jump about, while the captain's look betrayed a guilty conscience as he confessed that he'd neglected to mention one little activity they'd undertaken that might explain the arrival of the local authorities. He recounted how, after a protracted period of inactivity during which they'd drifted in heavy mist, he and his men (there were apparently no women aboard) happened to find themselves on what he called "a merry cur hunt." Though inexperienced at hunting animals over the side of a boat, they were eager to cast their nets and try their luck, having heard that a surefire way to grow rich would be to sell sweaters made from the marvellous hairs of the Afghan hound.

our eyes lit up at their cash-in-able furs. In no time at all our sea-sipping netters had caught a poop load of the knee-nipping setters. There was no question at all as we looked at our haul that these swell setters would help us sell sweaters.

"But the beautiful schnauzers were also snootiful bowsers, and soon their darling snouts were giving us snarling doubts. You couldn't step on the poop without being shit in the bins or crapped in the snotch, so it was almost a relief when the Talis came bounding aboard with their warrants and pedigrees and barking tickets and petting fees. They demanded their dog-due in vaunting dictums, portraying themselves as the daunting victims.

"Well, we'd soon had enough of these boring wankers who'd stormed our decks like warring bankers. And so to the sound of shattering barks, percussively nuanced by battering sharks, we shocked our assailants, each soggy dupe, by turning their hounds into doggy soup. But those curly-lipped pooches didn't get eaten, for the sharks were just dogfish, and now they paddled for shore, a bit weather-beaten, as the sea became a fog dish. Then sheathing their swords with their shiny tips, their masters returned to their tiny

---

Sure enough, these hounds were so abundant their numbers spilled over into the sea, where they were easily caught. Soon the poop deck was full of the wonderful beasts, and the crew's collective dream of becoming sweater tycoons looked on the verge of coming true.

The only problem was that the big dogs were rather nippy, to the point where one could hardly step onto the deck without being bit in the shins or snapped in the crotch. Despite their visions of glory and wealth, the captain and his charges were relieved when the officials and enforcers boarded their ship with the intention of reclaiming their property. In no uncertain legal terms, these officials demanded the return of the dogs and presented search warrants and identification papers for the missing hounds while issuing fines for disturbing the peace and petting without a permit. A list of rules and transgressions was read with impressive grandiloquence, leaving no question that the victims of this crime would not rest until justice was served. Having had enough of the whole business, the crew began tossing the blasted hounds overboard to the sharks, which had been thumping against the hull. They knew, of course—didn't they?—that the sharks were of a relatively harmless variety and that the dogs—despite the furious barking as they flew from the deck—would merely swim back to shore, shrouded though it had become by a sudden fog. At this point, the Afghanis could see that there was little hope of getting any money out of the trespassing rogues, so they sheathed their pens and swords and got back into their little boats—though one of them, by choice or decree, dove into the waves and swam behind the landward fleet of pooches, looking for all the world like a prissy transsexual mermaid.

ships—except for one who, like a foppish mermaid, swam in the wake the dogs' moppish fur made."

The captain took from his tan cap an articulated plume and began to gesture like a particulated loom. "Now free of yowly beasts and bowelly yeasts, free of debt peelers and pet dealers (who'd guarded their hairy wares like wary hares), it was time, as I said to my trusty carousers, to once again heal your soul and brave the seas!"

"Oh, seal your hole and save the breeze," muttered one of the crew. "I'm hungry."

"It was time," the quilled skipper waxed on, "to venture sanely with virgin sails upon the sea's vaulted sermon, time to censure vainly with surgeon veils upon the sea's salted vermin, time to—"

"Avast! Spare us the soppy cheese!" bellowed the first mate, a skilled quipper, "and get to the part with the choppy seas!"

The captain stood in a goutful daze, like a foggy duck in a doubtful gaze. Then, with the flourish of a magician pulling a rabbit out of a hat, or a behaviourist pulling a habit out of a rat, he came to his senses and resumed his tale.

Taking from his hat an intricate feather and making rhythmic yet disjointed movements, the captain paused in his narrative to reflect on the philosophical exhortation he'd given his men as they resumed their voyage to Bali. He quoted his own lofty and sentimental speech about the majesty and spiritual significance of the sea quest that lay ahead.

The crew, who were increasingly hungry and wanted his tedious reminiscence to reach its conclusion so they might be fed, managed to snap him out of his romantic digression by reminding him of the next dramatic misadventure they'd suffered on their trip: a storm that blew them off course and left them drifting at sea with little in the way of food to sustain them. It seems the journey was going so smoothly they started to enjoy themselves a little too much. During afternoon tea they became inebriated to such a degree they steered right into the tempest and were tossed helplessly around by the ferocity of its winds. When the seas settled, they found nothing left in the stores but a pot roast that was well past its prime—to the extent that, as the captain reflected bizarrely, it was about as gastronomically tempting as a cooked child. Still, they minced it into a sort of ground beef and managed to get it down, with possibly detrimental effects on their brains and teeth. The youngest of the sailors were particularly appalled, recounted the captain, but the others had laughed as they gagged and made humorous statements to the effect that it was really quite a delightful meal—just like sitting in the Pagan Stork pub back home and eating a delectable dish made of pig and deer.

One of the crew interjected to state acerbically that it had been more akin to sitting in the

"Right—the tempest! Well, after the cunning plan of our punning clan had failed, we set sail again and were on our way to Bali dutifully, but the voyage was going so well we began to dally beautifully. In fact, we got so sauced at tea we steered into a storm and got tossed at sea. We were flung about by those rig-ripping waters like a delirious gang of wig-whipping rotters. And worst of all, there was nothing left to eat but some leftover meat: an old potted roast that looked like an old rotted post. Well, that toasted rot was about as appetizing as a roasted tot, I can tell you. And though less awful when minced, still my men winced as they sat in bound grief and ate the ground beef. Drowning this ghoul—that is, downing this gruel—didn't do much for our mental dispositions, nor, for that matter, our dental mispositions. The newest members of our crew found this rare hazing somewhat hair-raising, but the rest of us cheerfully joked as we jeerfully choked that it was just like eating stag 'n' pork at the Pagan Stork."

"More like eating doggy food at the Foggy Dude," observed one of the crew.

The ensuing laughter was interrupted by the appearance of the

---

Foggy Dude and noshing a type of canned mush concocted in a factory to meet the basic nutritional requirements and culinary demands of a housebound cur.

The lighthouse erupted in laughter, and one can imagine even Shauna and the sentry, if he were to overhear from his post, having a good chuckle at the witticism.

Their hysterics were cut short by the appearance of Ronna, a lovely young woman who'd been hired to do light housekeeping (a sort of mer-maid, so to speak), assist with chores and care for the sick animals taken in by the master of the lighthouse. One could be excused for wondering if Ronna's fair appearance factored into her attaining this new position, for her previous work experience consisted primarily of evangelizing about the Christian messiah and setting cheese on fire (though, to be fair, she had achieved considerable renown in that latter pursuit—especially in Japan, where her virtuosic torching of Greek cheese had caused the culinary press to stand up and shout, "Opa!").

Ronna set down on the coffee table, next to the small furry mammals, a dish of the pressed and fermented milk curds for which she was known and a thick strand of delectable hard buttery candy that softens when chewed (perhaps not the wisest choice of dessert for a bunch of scurvy dogs whose dental condition was fragile at best).

"Please chatter!" encouraged Ronna, but an uncomfortable silence prevailed, for this otherwise charming maiden (proselytizing aside) had spent so much time in the company of pungent cheeses that her rank aura left the room speechless.

The captain, ignorant of the source of this fetor or perhaps just oblivious to decorum,

fetching Ronna, recently employed by the lighthouse keeper (who was off visiting his cousin, the kitehouse leaper) to do light housekeeping, assist with chores and tend to the retching fauna. Until then, she'd spent her life jittering about cheeses while—for this "purdy creature" was also a curdy preacher—chittering about Jesus. A real Shire and brimstone minister of Munster, Ronna could flambée boule like a Bombay fool, and her saganaki was the talk of Nagasaki. Setting upon the coffee table a toffee cable and a cheese platter, she encouraged the suddenly quiet guests to "Please chatter!"

The stooping wench emitted such a whooping stench, the captain couldn't help but ask, "Does anyone smell socks—er, I mean," seeing that his reference to the cheddar reek had given her a redder cheek, "sell smocks? I need a tall smock for a small talk I plan to give on the subject of...of...The Fire Drill: Is It But a Dire Frill?"

At that moment, a willing swine darted in and started swilling wine.

"That white rhino is a right wino," commented the first mate.

"It's not a rhino," corrected the bosun, "just a sweaty pig having a petty swig."

---

broke the silence by asking, "Does anyone smell socks?" Noticing that Ronna blushed at this question, the captain backtracked and pretended he'd made a slip of the tongue and had actually meant to ask if there were any merchants of loose protective overalls among them, claiming unconvincingly that he needed such a garment for a lecture he intended to deliver on the subject of whether or not fire drills were crucial but insignificant exercises.

The social awkwardness of the moment was boisterously dispelled by an eager pig who dashed into the room and began guzzling wine, which had evidently been set out for guests. The first mate mistook the pig for a white rhinoceros and commented, with some degree of awe, that it was quite an alcoholic. The boatswain corrected him, saying that it was just a perspiring swine enjoying a little quaff. Then the navigator chimed in, making the rather startling admission that, regardless of what type of animal it was, the sight of its bald hindquarters was giving him serious thoughts of homosexual bestiality as a means to end his circumstantial celibacy.

Just as he was about to wager that the sow was game for sexual intercourse, a cry of pain pierced the air: Ronna had lost her step and fallen on a novelty telephone in the shape of a rabbit, striking her ulnar nerve in the process. She had no idea what had happened, and the first thing that crossed her mind was that a pyromaniac must have somehow fractured her arm near the elbow—perhaps a Freudian assumption best left to the experts, or perhaps just a recognition that she herself (a "pyro" of cheese by profession) was responsible for the accident. In any case, she immediately picked up the receiver and tearfully bellowed her account

"I don't care if it's a groundhog drinking hound grog," confessed the navigator, who was also the mail sender and the sail mender. "My male state has been in such a stalemate that that critter's hairless butt is starting to look as inviting as a bearless hut on a stormy night. I'll bet you four bucks that boar—"

A shriek from across the room rent the air: Ronna had tripped and smacked her funny bone on the novelty bunny phone. A moment after falling on the bone she was bawling on the phone to her chiropractor, wailing that some pyro cracked her (though seeing there was no flame on the bone she should surely have put the blame on the phone).

To cheer her up, the captain, in his maturated sanity, pulled out his cellphone and pretended he was speaking to a saturated manatee. This talking charade soon became a shocking tirade, prompting some of his audience to dub the captain a tireless wit, and others to say that he was something much less flattering. The mock call over, that tragic mick did a magic trick and produced a bandicoot from a candy boot, but still Ronna sobbed. Next, he tried to amuse her by poking her ribs with a pool cue he'd carved from a

---

of the incident to her chiropractor.

With a mind to take her thoughts off the pain and perhaps even bring her a snicker or two, the captain—clearly suffering, or enjoying, the effects of age-related cognitive deterioration—took out his small wireless telephone and simulated a conversation with a drunken manatee. Some of those present felt that his histrionics had grown excessive when he began viciously berating the poor sea beast, but others professed to enjoy his unflagging waggish humour. When the call ended—did the manatee hang up on him?—the lamentable Irishman (who was, in fact, half English) performed an act of legerdemain by extracting a marsupial insectivore native to Australia and New Guinea from a boot-shaped confection. So far nothing was working, for despite his doting foolery Ronna continued to weep. His next tack—perhaps a little desperate and juvenile for a man of his years—was to try to elicit a giggle by jabbing at her ribcage with a billiards stick he'd crafted from a splendid wooden bench once reserved for lower primates at a certain temple where agents of prostitutes worshipped. Seeing that even this effort failed to draw a smile, the captain, that predicament-solving seeker of cargo, decided it was time to pull out all the stops with his ever-popular consciousness-altering one-man silent theatrical production of a rather objectionable comedic piece he called The Haughty Doleful Whore Behind the Dotty Holeful Door. Well, that silent thespian of an old seaman figuratively removed the soft layered rocks that were weighing him down and vigorously wiggled his bottom, adroitly parading his dilapidated antique body like a horny, slovenly, burlesque-dancing, geriatric matron. While this little show, true to the tradition of mime, employed no

cool pew that had once been the perch for chimps at the Church for Pimps. Still no laughter, so it was time for that bind-mending stow-shopper to bring down the lighthouse with his mind-bending show-stopper—a mime routine called The Haughty Doleful Whore Behind the Dotty Holeful Door. Well, that mime of an ancient mariner took out his shale and shook out his tail, rippingly strutting his dumpy old frame like a strippingly rutting frumpy old dame. But while phonically silent, this pantomime was still rather sonically violent, for the captain was prone to a condition he called "the vapours."

"That's a class act," muttered one of his crew as the captain's ass clacked.

The spunky schoonerist soldiered on—a bold hack who wouldn't hold back—but no artful factor of the ailing farce could redeem this fartful actor of the failing arse. A further disgrace finally ended the show when its most artistically constructed illusion—the barrier of the door—was vulgarly shattered by the derrière of the boar, who, having downed the Barolo and finished the Brie, staggered backwards through the invisible partition like a fumbling buck.

---

verbal expression, it still had its pronounced sonic aspect owing to a gastrointestinal condition that flared up at the most inconvenient times.

"That's a class act," muttered one of the crew with regard to the captain's percussively flatulent disruption of his own determinedly silent antics. To make matters worse, the act's most deftly articulated theme—the spotted door full of holes—was disgracefully demolished by the bum of the pig who, after finishing off the wine and cheese, tottered backwards through the imaginary structure like a male deer suffering from nervous clumsiness.

A member of the audience—a crew member, I should say—shattered the silence by asking tactlessly if there mightn't be a hot beverage to follow their light repast.

At point the captain, who seemed to take life very lightly and art very seriously, went berserk, tearing at his shirt and emitting what could perhaps best be described as a "mirth bark"—the sort of irrational and complex bellow typically heard only in times of celebratory debauchery. In doing so, he exposed a splotch on his chest—a bit of God's own graffiti in the shape of a manta or "devil" ray. He began to snap his jaws and blither, raving incantatorily as he stomped about the room in pursuit of the pig. The more the pig eluded him, the more his men seemed to enjoy the show. When he finally caught his porcine prey, he landed on it with such force it seemed a cabin and some large rocks had been responsible for its collapse.

The situation was worse than it looked for both the captain and the pig because Ronna, trying to get out of her painful funk, had begun mopping the floor with a bed rag—and that was the very spot where the two went down. The surface was so slippery with suds that they

The silence that followed was broken by one of the crew: "Um...the cheese and toffee was great—do you happen to have any teas and coffee?"

The captain, exasperated, uttered a sort of revel day mirth bark and tore at his shirt, exposing a devil ray birthmark. Then he chomped as he ranted and he romped as he chanted, charging at the boar for barging at the door. (Always happy to bet on both fun and war, the crew placed odds of one and four.)

Chasing the pig, the captain discovered, was like trying to catch a greyhound in a hayground, but after a fair run (which his men thought rare fun) he actually managed to fell the sucker.

The beast went down as if a shack and boulders had fallen on its back and shoulders—but it didn't stop, for it had landed on the very spot where Ronna, still moping and sopping, had taken a bed rag from a red bag and begun soaping and mopping the floor. The pig and the captain slid on the thickening suds, flew from the room and under the rail, hovered fleetingly in the fog light like a couple of lumberjacks in a log fight, then plummeted—with sickening thuds—to the ground far below.

---

slid right out of the room, under the guard rail and out into mid-air where they appeared momentarily frozen in suspended animation, like the photographic image of two loggers battling in a luminous mist. The sound that swiftly succeeded their descent was horrible to the ears: a nauseating double thump that left Ronna in stunned supplication to her god and Shauna in serious disequilibrium, her complexion the colour of aluminum that has undergone replication by means of a digital imaging device. Speechless, she swooned towards the sea and dropped at the feet of the boatswain, who was anxiously looking for his dear captain in the direction of the wind. The small furry insectivore leapt about with evident distress, perhaps picking up in some subtle way best defined and articulated by specialists in animal behaviour the funereal sadness of the crew as they morbidly sobbed at the surely fatal mishap that had befallen their leader.

The boatswain, with a look in his eyes as if they'd been selected from a package of frozen bovine orbs in a supermarket meat bin, hailed him as a god of the oceans, a Neptune. The sentry bayed like a rueful doofus and, by way of honouring the pig and the captain, blasted a round of ammunition out to sea. He mistakenly (though, under the circumstances, rather aptly) referred to the fallen skipper as Captain Ineptune. Had the captain been an incompetent singer who couldn't carry a tune, and had the sentry and others been forced to hear the spew of such a crooner, perhaps a name like that would have served as a fond tribute to a "king of seas" who could only "sing off keys"! But I digress. The significant thing about the marksman's gesture, from at least a literary if not an ethical perspective, is that he happened to shoot a passing alba-

Ronna, shocked, began to pray while Shauna rocked and began to sway, her tanned skin now pale as scanned tin. Glazed and dumb and lurching seaward, she fell at the feet of the bosun, dazed and glum and searching leaward. The shrew leapt worriedly as the crew wept luridly, knowing their captain would voyage no more.

"He was a king of the seas—a real Neptune," sobbed the fraught bosun, with a look in his eyes like they'd been bought frozen.

Then the sentry howled like a sorry galoot and fired off a round in a gory salute (he slaughtered an albatross gliding nearby). "To Captain Ineptune and his flying pig!" the poor sinner brayed outside the doorway where Ronna, the Boursiner, prayed.

Shauna half-rose with a queasy cheer, then Ronna—still propped in her stare—stopped in her prayer to ask, of no one in particular, "Who was that cheesy queer?"

The first mate turned to Ronna, that sizzler of cheese, and spoke of his captain, that chiseller of seas: "He was born with the mark of a beast called the manta, so his parents named him Ray, but to all those who knew him, and some who did not, he was simply known as—"

---

tross—an inauspicious act, to say the least.

Meanwhile, Ronna (who, by the way, makes an excellent Boursin cheese) was standing nearby in the doorway, still praying away.

In response to the sentry's odd toast, Shauna half-rose from the floor to offer a nauseous hurrah. Then Ronna stopped praying at the sudden realization that she had no idea of the identity of the man for whose safety or soul she was petitioning. Who, she asked (rather in the spirit of a fundamentalist theatre critic), was that "cheesy queer"?

Ignoring the epithet, the first mate launched into a pointlessly convoluted account of how the captain—christened Ray by his parents—came to be known as Jack. Before he could get very far, a painful yelp (sounding much like a piratical greeting, and nearly a phonetic reversal of the captain's original name) drowned him out. The yelp, of course, belonged to none other than the captain—up from his fall and in from a fresh downpour, battered and bleeding but obviously very much alive.

The seamen were ecstatic at the sight of their leader, and true to form the small furry insectivore twirled with apparent delight.

The navigator asked the question on everyone's mind: how did the captain survive his dire tumble?

The answer to that question can be explained by a combination of chaos theory, synchronicity conjecture and Fortean philosophy: sensitive dependence on initial conditions combined with an acausal connecting principle and a textbook example of the damnedest thing

"Yar!" came a yelp of roaring pain, as a figure stepped in from the pouring rain.

"—Jack!"

The seamen erupted in joy, for the old bleeder who stood before them was none other than their bold leader.

"But, Captain, how did you survive that drastic spill?" asked the navigator, as the shrew twirled about like a spastic drill.

"Well, as I looked down I saw that pig billow in its fall—so full of Boarsin and Boardeaux it made a nice big pillow (one size fits all). The downward spin scared me but the pig's skin spared me. So I'm saved, but—" here the captain, part limey boor, paused for effect "—*blimey*—sore!"

"Praise the Lord," said Ronna, "but what about our slimy boar?"

"Oh, his crumbling bacon was saved by a bumbling kraken that washed up onshore. He slid from that squid like a mail truck on trail muck and we both hit the breakwall with all the force of a wake brawl—hence the thud and the blood."

Just then the keeper of the lighthouse—a Mr. Albert Ross—flew in, back from his cousin's kitehouse where he'd been sharing drinks

---

happening. Had the pig not gorged itself on cheese and wine (especially the rich Boursin and heavy Bordeaux), it might not have attained the essential suppleness and girth to provide such a non-aerodynamic cushion for the captain who, fortuitously, was falling directly above it, and if not for the singular occurrence of a giant squid washing up onshore on that very spot where they were about to fall, the pig would almost certainly have been fatally wounded. So it was a confluence of factors in an improbable sequence that saved the two. Which is not to say their landing was entirely cushy: Nature and Chance had done what they could to make their meeting with the earth relatively comfortable; however, humanity had erected a concrete wall to lessen the force of wave against shore, and it was this into which the pig and sailor thudded after sliding from the back of the slippery kraken.

The fall seemed to have further disintegrated the captain's personality: one moment the English half of his character would dominate and he'd describe his pain by the use of a British slang term denoting surprise and alarm, the next his Irish half would take over and he'd attempt to convey the intensity of his impact with the wall in an analogy referencing an Irish post-mortem ritual.

The captain had just finished relating the essentials of his fall and rise when the keeper of the lighthouse returned, soaking wet and in a foul mood. Mr. Albert Ross—and it seems no one commented on the curious fact that one albatross would plummet moments before another "albertross" would rise—was back from his cousin's kitehouse (whatever that may be), where he'd been sharing drinks with two psychiatrists who liked to gamble. They'd chal-

with two daring shrinks who'd challenged him to an oyster-eating contest.

"Great shucking fit!" he exclaimed, slamming the door. "It's raining bats and hogs out there!"

"It wasn't a bat," corrected the bosun, "just a natty bird blasted by a batty nerd."

Keeper Ross spun around with a look of awed shock, like a shod auk in Victorian sandals who'd been set upon by sick Taurean vandals.

"What the fiddling duck is going on here?" he squawked.

"He seems like a pheasant plucker, doesn't he," said the navigator.

"I don't know about that," replied the first mate, "but if he mistook an albatross for a bat he's definitely not a bird watcher—more of a word botcher, by the sounds of it."

The keeper's gaze darted about the room like a hill grouse being chased by a chef at a grill house.

"And where's that busy ditch with the turkey pits I hired to mend the souls in my hawks? Where is she—out staking a troll with some

---

lenged him to an oyster-eating contest and it appears that all the shucking had proven a little overwhelming for the birdlike man, especially given his state of intoxication.

The odd thing about the lighthouse keeper was that he had a manner of speaking whereby he involuntarily jumbled words and phrases, sometimes to mildly comic effect. This verbal sabotage of meaning frequently spared those within hearing range of some exceptionally vile oaths and invectives, as well as some rather repulsive expressions of chauvinism and racism.

Not only was he oafish, but he may have been a bit of a birdbrain as well. For example, the first statement he made upon entering the interior of the lighthouse was "It's raining bats and hogs out there." Now, if he was saying what he meant in this case, he was evidently—as the boatswain pointed out—misidentifying an albatross as a bat. Maybe it was just his boozy stupefaction, or maybe it *was* raining bats. We know it was raining hogs—well, one at least.

As for his sexism and crapulence, so enamoured and amused by his conduct was Ronna that she seemed quite willing to overlook both, even beseeching others, in a momentary spasm of linguistic contagion, to not *b*ind her *m*oss.

Shauna was less inclined to overlook his behaviour, though given her almost existentially detached nature she wasn't going to wade too far into the issue, letting the matter go with what may have been a derogatory faecal reference cleverly parodying the lighthouse keeper's own flusterphonic style.

The captain, on the other hand, was incensed enough by the lighthouse keeper's rudeness to Ronna that he proclaimed himself ready to fight, were it not for the fact of his being a

dairy hick when she should be here trashing my monk jail and lurking the womb?"

Ronna emerged from the crowd holding a shrill chimp she'd taught to chill shrimp. Amused by her employer's way of speaking in twirling syntax with demented sense, she began to guffaw like a swirling tin sax with cemented dents.

"Don't bind my moss," she began, before doubling over baftly as her laughter bubbled over daftly.

"Donna, my rear! Why, the gore pearl is flickering so snakily she's tossed her lung!"

Indeed, as the keeper observed, the poor girl was snickering so flakily she'd lost her tongue, but finally she managed to speak: "I mean, don't mind my boss—it's just that when he's in a drinking stupor he can be a real stinking drooper."

"He is a tit of a bird, isn't he," added Shauna.

"If I weren't a guest here, I'd fight that brute," said the captain.

"Oh, don't bite that fruit," said the first mate, but it was too late: the captain had found in the pocket of his trousers—the ones with "Known on the Sea" sewn on the knee—an old tannic mango, so

---

guest and therefore bound by certain rules of etiquette (I will not venture to surmise which half of his personality was in place at the time of that observation). Instead, the captain found himself happily distracted by the discovery of a tropical fruit that must have inhabited his trousers pocket for a considerable span of time, having by appearances long ago expired there and continued its residency as a fermenting corpse.

The first mate seemed shocked but not surprised when the captain lifted the ancient fruit to his mouth, and his advice—which clearly would not have been heeded anyway—came too late. "Oh, don't bite that fruit," he said, as if addressing, through a closed window or at too great a distance to be heard, a young child about to put a worm in his mouth.

The fruit was indeed so potently alcoholic that after only one bite, and despite his years of imbibing the most inebriating liquids concocted by man in the world's most depraved ports, the captain commenced to fling himself about the room in a hyperactive solo execution of a Latin American ballroom dance marked by melodramatic postures, extreme rhythmic shifts and abrupt pauses.

The crew—who adored their skipper but were often either frustrated by or in hysterics over his deportment—were shaking with laughter. And the small furry insectivore was a-tremble—but, again, one would have to be educated in the science and psychology of animal behaviour to divine whether that was from nervousness at the confusing outburst of energy in its surroundings or from a type of psychic or visceral resonance with the jocularity emanating from the crew, with whom it had spent time at sea and thereby perhaps "entrained" to their

highly fermented that after only one bite he danced about the room in a manic tango.

The shrew began to quake as the crew began to shake with laughter. Even the rotten keeper, usually grim as a cotton reaper, joined in. Then the sluggish onerous sentry made his luggish sonorous entry, droning like a Middle Age monk and moaning like a middle-age drunk. Hoisting his gun he shot the crew a crazy look as he caught the shrew like a lazy crook and plopped it on the chimp's back. The monkey's jaw dropped in surprise, till its mouth hung wide as a nodding junkie's maw. But Ronna had trained him to follow the Golden Rule, to share each meal, even olden gruel. So, as the Saviour himself might have done, he lifted a shrimp from his bowl of prawns and held it aloft like a pole of bronze. Then the shrew on the chimp began to chew on the shrimp, and soon the whole crew joined in, grabbing at the cold prawns with all the manners of paroled cons.

"Follow the food rules, you rude fools!" preached Ronna. Then, hearing at the door a low knock, she turned and shouted, "Come in, there's no lock!"

---

emotional frequencies (amateur speculation, of course), *or* a third and admittedly more preposterous hypothesis: maybe the creature, in its mysterious way, simply thought the captain was funny as he danced convulsively about, bloodied and tattered, twisting and twirling in paroxysms of flamboyant passion, romantically dipping an invisible partner at breakneck speed, shifting to petrifaction at the momentary discontinuance of imaginary music. Probably, though, it was just agitated by the noise in the room.

The lighthouse keeper, who is usually grim as someone who reaps the soft white fibres surrounding the seeds of a subtropical plant used to make textiles, also laughed.

Then that sly dolt of a sentry stepped inside, droning like a medieval religious ascetic and moaning like a dipsomaniac who was no longer young but not yet old.

He glanced psychotically at the crew, then, in the manner of a lackadaisical thief, scooped up the small furry insectivore and plunked it on the back of a chimpanzee who was holding a bowl of shellfish Ronna had taught it to frigidify for consumption.

The degree to which this unexpected visitation surprised the monkey was evidenced by the sudden dropping of its jaw, so that it hung as slack as the mouth of someone experiencing the cessation of addictive craving upon the intravenous administration of a drug notorious for its stupendous opiate effect. But Ronna had somehow taught the simian at least one of the tenets of Christianity—that you should treat others as you would have them treat you. So, in emulation of Jesus, the trained primate held up a shrimp—as if it were a bronze pole—and offered it to the small furry insectivore. The odds of the creature, accustomed to a diet of

"What's with the canned trout and the jealous zoo?" asked Keeper Ross, seeing two officers of the law step into the room.

"Hello, officers," said Ronna, waving her hands behind her back like a bordello's door bellows, "I hope you're having an enjoyable evening. What brings you to our lusty old fighthouse—I mean, our fusty old lighthouse?"

"Oh, don't worry about the noise," said Officer Faerber, lifting his hat to reveal a rug made of bear fur. "We didn't rush ashore to make you shush a roar. And as for our evening…well, let's just say it was a fun night until the nun fight."

"And then that band sank in a sandbank," added Officer Goldbloom.

"That was just before we found that vendor slain with a knife to his slender vein."

"Yeah, an old guy with a shop called the Gold Eye—sold everything from popcorn to cop porn."

"After that, things got even worse: next we had to wade through a dull bog on a rain trek to rescue a bulldog from a train wreck. He was real bucking fighter, too, not to mention a—"

---

insects, ever having consumed shrimp before are slim, but it took to the experience with relish, possibly because it had had little to eat for some time.

The crew seemed to take this as a cue to forget their manners and dove in as one, grabbing at the cold little sea monsters with all the refinement of hungry prisoners who'd been let out for the day.

Ronna admonished them, but the feeding frenzy continued noisily—seafood, we must conclude, being more appealing to these voyagers than cheese.

A knock at the door proved to be two police officers—one a swarthy Teuton and the other an orthodox follower of the Judaic faith. Ronna greeted them while frantically waving her hands behind her back, as if to simulate a two-handled air-blowing bag affixed for unknown reasons to a brothel's door. She expressed a wish that their evening was pleasurable, then inquired—obviously affected by the tumbled jock of her employer—as to what brought them to "our lusty old fighthouse."

Officer Faerber divined Ronna's intent with the posterior flapping gesture and assured her, as he removed his cap and exposed a toupee made of fur from a large mammal inclined to eating berries, honey and occasionally humans, that he and his partner had not rushed ashore (for they were a special branch of the constabulary working closely with the Coast Guard) to make them keep the noise down. With regard to how their evening was going, he said it had been fine—prior to the brawl that broke out among women of a religious community living under vows of poverty, chastity and devotion to the Lord.

"Gentlemen," interrupted Ronna, assuming the stance of a jock when a jock teases, "if you're not here about the noise, why are you here—surely not to talk Jesus?"

"Actually, miss," said Officer Goldbloom, "we had a report that some stoned cocksucker shot a dolphin."

"I can honestly say," said Ronna honestly, "that no one here shot a dolphin—not even Golding the Hun over there holding the gun."

The sentry smiled like a ghoulish Buddha who'd just devoured a boulish Gouda.

"Well, sorry to bother you nice folks," said Officer Goldbloom, doffing one of his caps, then suddenly recalling a bit of trivia about a writer known for his bold gloom: "Say, did you know that snow peas made Poe sneeze?"

Before anyone could think to answer, the keeper of this high ribald haven—somewhat sobered but still swaying about like a wry highballed raven—piped up to say goodnight. "Now, I hate to drift off like a farting dog," he said, "but tepee slime is upon me and I'm off to catch warty finks."

"The story of my life," said an awkward Officer Faerber, feeling

---

Officer Goldbloom chimed in by mentioning the next incident that had required their attention: the sinking of a musical ensemble in a ridge of sand rising out of the water.

The chronological summary continued with Officer Faerber's reference to their having next discovered a merchant who had been murdered—and here the dark Rhine poet showed himself in Faerber—"with a knife to his slender vein." He was an elderly fellow, according to Goldbloom, who had a little store that sold everything from maize kernels meant to be exploded by heat and then snacked upon to books and videos featuring police in such a way as to inspire sexual excitement.

The night, said Faerber, got even worse following that episode, when they had to wade through a dreary tract of wet muddy land to rescue from train wreckage a squat, wrinkly-faced dog with powerful jaws. Despite their benign heroics, the dog put up quite a fight during the rescue operation and proved himself a nasty biter too—though the officer failed to get out that last detail before Ronna interrupted to imply, with a slight impatience in her voice and an almost taunting posture, that he should skip all that and get to the point of their visit. Though she might have liked otherwise, she presumed that they had not climbed the lighthouse steps to discuss the Son of God.

Goldbloom responded by announcing that they'd received a report about a drug-addled practitioner of fellatio having shot a dolphin.

Ronna may or may not have known about the sentry's having shot a gentleman disguised as such a creature, but in either case she answered truthfully (so far as we know) that no one

erect from the reeling effect of being so high up—or perhaps it was the stinky whiff of fair Ronna and her rare fauna that made his winkie stiff.

"Just one other thing..." said Officer Goldbloom, like a niggling judge, as he gave his partner a jiggling nudge.

"Oh yes," said Officer Faerber. "Would you mind turning off that light? It's shining on the boats and we're concerned about a crash on our rocks."

The captain, having found his inlaid—or is that inlain?—satin flagon dry after flitting about like an insane Latin dragonfly, had gone on a careless hunt in search of liquid treasure. Exploring the most remote nooks and crannies of the lighthouse, where only crooks and nannies had gone before, this prince of the ocean found not even a rinse of the potion he sought. What he did find were the spoor and faeces of many foreign species, including a brute of a kitten that this coot of a Briton dressed in a mod ascot and pronounced his odd mascot.

And now, pushing his way through the crowd on the back of a

---

there—not even the gun-toting guardsman—had done such a thing. As she referenced him, the sentry smiled like a fiendish corpse-eating pacifist master of a transcendental Eastern religion who had just consumed a ball-like portion of yellow-rinded Dutch cheese.

Tipping his uniform hat but leaving his skullcap in situ, Officer Goldbloom apologized for the bother and made to leave when he happened to recall a bit of literary trivia he thought the assembly might enjoy. It was regarding an allergic reaction said to afflict Edgar Allan Poe, causing him to violently expel air from his nostrils and mouth whenever he came in contact with a certain leguminous vegetable recognizable by its slender translucent pod.

There was a moment of tranquility as Ronna, Shauna, the sentry, lighthouse keeper Ross and the crew, having finished the shrimp, contemplated this marvellous fact, a little unsure perhaps as to what response might do justice to such a fascinating intellectual tidbit.

The spell of awe and befuddlement was soon burst by the master of that sometimes coarse and lively sanctuary-in-the-sky. Somewhat sobered by the appearance of the police but still swaying like a large black crow with an ironic and sarcastic sensibility, tipsy from imbibing mixed drinks, Mr. Ross excused himself for bed, announcing, after his own style, that he hated to drift off like a darting fog but sleepy time was upon him and he was off to catch forty winks.

Officer Faerber, who had understood him to say that he was off to catch "warty finks," rejoined—with some distraction arising from a temporary condition of penile engorgement and stiffening resulting from either the vertiginous altitude or a hormonally charged olfactory reaction to the peculiar pungency of Ronna and the unusual creatures in her care—by saying

shoving leopard, the captain collected his crew—like a loving shepherd gathering his doting flock—and led them down to the floating dock where their schooner lay moored.

On their way to the ship they encountered two vocal lawyers whom they mistook for local voyeurs. The men—prosecution attorneys moonlighting as exterminators—were debating flat fees for eliminating fat fleas and whether or not to charge treble hours for rebel towers such as the one that loomed before them: a lighthouse with encrested features full of all manner of infested creatures. The sign on their van read: *Leacock & Keylock—Mitigating Lice and Litigating Mice Our Specialty.*

The captain, first to board ship, spotted a garish stowaway and fixed him with a starish "Go away." This had no effect on the strange man in the dolphin suit, so the tiny Brit turned to his crew and demanded, "Who is this briny tit?"

"My name," said the stowaway, "is Francis 'Frank' Raleigh and I'm the victim of a rather rank folly. You see, I'd been invited to a mask ball at a Basque mall and I decided to ask our maid what I should wear to this masquerade. She suggested I attend as a court-

---

that it was "the story of my life."

"One other thing..." said Officer Goldbloom, rather in the manner of an overly particular official who decides results in legal matters or competitions. As a mnemonic prompt, he lightly jabbed Officer Faerber's chubby ribs, snapping him out of his unfocused discomfiture.

"Oh yes," said Officer Faerber, recalling the matter they'd discussed as they approached the tower from sea. "Would you mind turning off that light?" He explained their concern that a nautical disaster might occur—"a crash on our rocks," to be specific—should the beam interfere with seafarers' ability to safely navigate the waters upon which it fell (just a safety precaution). As we see later, the light remained on. Presumably, the job of illuminating the officers as to the purpose of a lighthouse fell to Ronna.

The captain had snuck off to look for booze in the far recesses of the lighthouse. Instead, he found the tracks and excrement of various exotic animals. It was on the back of one of these—a leopard given to pushiness—that he rode back to his crew, drawing them together as would an affectionate overseer of woolly grass-eating mammals gather his excessively fond herd. He then led them down the spiralling stairs of the lighthouse to the buoyant pier where his ship (which for no apparent reason was called *The Spooner*) lay anchored and tethered.

Along their route they passed a couple of noisy legal practitioners who at first appeared to be peeping toms. On some metaphoric whim, no doubt, these courtroom predators were operating a side business as paid destroyers of insects and rodents. Their confidence and

ly porpoise so we thus attired my portly corpus. Having granted a night off to my bodyguard—a Sherpa from Persia who'd gone to hear some gaudy bard—I set off from our yacht alone. When my dinghy snagged and began to decompose on a rock, all I could do was swim for shore in the hope I might recompose on a dock. That's when my plan of frolicking among sinful gentry was shot down by a ginful sentry—a coltish vassal in that voltish castle over there. Yes, some sassy ass of an asinine assassin ass-assassinated me. Though the bullet that marred me merely grazed my butt, it may as well have braised my gut, for I sank like a jogging lamb in a logging jam. Fortunately, I managed to grab hold of a stretcherous length of cable attached to your weighty anchors, which I clutched with the lecherous strength of eighty wankers. I then pulled myself to safety above the greedy waves and weedy graves of drowned seamen.

"There was, by the way, another victim who was not so lucky: some loony sobster who was wailing and waving a sail that I think read something like SAVE THE SUNNI LOBSTER."

"So I take it you want a lift back to the yacht," said the navigator,

---

expertise in this secondary field may have been less than infallible, as the promotional slogan on their vehicle stated that one of their specialties was in merely "mitigating" a certain form of parasitic insect and that the other—relying heavily on their professional background—was in serving legal notices to small furry pests whose numbers tend to prevail despite much more forcible means of eviction such as poisoning and trapping. They seemed to be preparing for the job of ridding the lighthouse of its multiple infestations associated with its resident wildlife.

Upon boarding the ship, the captain noticed a gaudy trespasser who would have been decadently attired even without the dolphin costume. It was, of course, the first of the two unlucky fellows presumed to have been ruthlessly murdered by the sentry. He had, in fact, suffered only a surface wound by virtue of all but one of the marksman's bullets—and that one striking obliquely—missing their target. It was not the first misfortune of this odd gentleman's evening: the reason he'd been swimming for shore is that the dinghy in which he'd embarked from his yacht had ripped on a rock and deflated. Normally, he would have been accompanied by his bodyguard—a Nepalese mountain guide who had lived for some time in Iran—but the fellow had been granted a free evening to attend a poetry reading by an author whose ornate personal style reflected the rich aesthetic tradition of his homeland. His purpose in leaving his ship—and this explains the dolphin outfit, as well—had been to attend a fancy masquerade party at an indoor shopping complex exclusively featuring shops marketing products and services from a serene yet politically tumultuous region of northern Spain which extends along the

a man accustomed, from many undignified sea tours, to unsignified detours.

"I'm not fussy, really," replied Frank, absently adjusting his dorsal fin by tugging at his hole. "Wherever you happen to be going is fine, as long as the locals don't shoot me and there's tea with crumpets; and of course when I soak my crumpets in tea it's always nice to hear trumpets in key, so as long as there's a quay with trumpets—Gnostical trumpets—and maybe some Saxon flutes played by nautical strumpets in flaxen suits, I'll be quite content; as long as there are Fijian wigs and Ouija and figs, and—oh!—some of those Turkish mints with the murkish tints; as long as I can sip Vanilla Mirandas on Manila verandahs with Geishan hosts and Haitian ghosts; as long as there are Iberian lynx I can sketch with Liberian inks, and Brahmans in shambles and shamans in brambles chewing bollocksome frondage that transports them into a sort of frolicsome bondage; as long as there are pine forts where I can drink fine ports after Incan meals of mink and eels; as long as there are..."

When he got to the part about sherry-showered boars roasting on berry-bowered shores, up trotted the pig itself.

Pyrenees into France. Alas, his hopes of indulging in some naughty fun with the class of people nearest the aristocracy were dashed when a glancing shot scraped his posterior. Despite the superficiality of the injury, he sank like a meek quadruped trotting on a congestion of logs bobbing in a lake whose arboreal shores were being harvested by the lumber industry. It was only thanks to a burst of energy, which seemed to be sparked by a kind of autoerotic fury in the face of imminent death, that he—Frank was his name—managed to hoist himself to safety via the anchor rope of the schooner. He also mentioned, in case the captain or his crew might care, that he was not the only one inconvenienced by sniping: a blubbering ninny who, seeing him splash about like a dying cetacean after the dinghy's demise, had come to his rescue with a banner Frank mistakenly recalled as having read SAVE THE SUNNI LOBSTER, had been fatally shot.

The navigator seemed less interested in the particulars of the stowaway's tale than in whatever additional bother his presence might entail. "So I take it you want a lift back to the yacht," he said, his perfunctory tone betraying a hint of weary resignation.

Frank replied that he was happy to tag along wherever they might be going. "I'm not fussy," he said, before elaborately inventorying the extraordinary and exotic sensory delights he would modestly anticipate along the way. Just as he specified something about a hog feast, the same pig that had fallen from the lighthouse scampered up the ramp and joined them on deck.

Seeing the pig, the pushy leopard made a charge straight for it. The captain clung for dear life as the ungainly cat took off in clumsy pursuit, chasing the boar across the beautifully fili-

The bumbling feline, with the captain still astraddle, made a fumbling beeline for the pearly swine and chased it across the swirly pine of the deck. The pig let out a squeal and began to wobble while the first mate and the navigator grabbed the wheel and began to squabble about where to sail next.

And as the leopard gave the boar a shove and the lighthouse shone on the shore above, a tourist stepped aboard the ship, with a splendid plan for a nautical trip.

"I hear Siberia is nice this time of year," said Shauna, "if you go by Syria."

THE END

---

greed grain of the floorboards. The squeal of the pig as it tottered on the brink of exhaustion (really, it had had quite a day) rose above the voices of the first mate and the navigator, who were clutching the wheel and arguing—for the captain himself was engaged—about what course to set.

It was into this mad chaos that Shauna, after descending the steps of the lighthouse, cast her lot. This newest member of the crew proposed a voyage that, while quite impossible, was no more outlandish than many previous seafaring escapades aboard *The Spooner*.

And so they set sail again, this strange society—but of their fate beyond this point we know nothing. We can only hope that Shauna quickly found her sea legs and is free of nausea, that the pig and the leopard are getting along without serious mischief, that the navigator has chanced now and again upon a lawful cure for celibacy, that the captain's antics have not endangered the lives of his crew or himself, and that the winds of delirious fortune will blow ever favourably the sails of their little ship.

THE END

ACKNOWLEDGMENTS

The author expresses his fond and enduring gratitude to Stuart Ross, whose significant contribution in acquiring and bringing to life these texts marks twenty-five years of enjoyable friendship and collaboration. Thanks as well to Mansfield publisher Denis De Klerck—a man in his right field!

"Manta Ray Jack and the Crew of the Spooner" is an homage to the Reverends Dodgson and Spooner—who "sought it with thimbles" and thought it with symbols—and to Dr. Seuss, too. All spoonerisms (though some may already have been discovered) are originals by the author, apart from four: thanks to Dale Zentner for "the souls in my hawks," Dr. David Naylor for "a word botcher," William Davison for "an old guy" and the Rev. William Archibald Spooner himself for his "shoving leopard."

For distending their aphorisms, the author (alas, too late) extends his apologies to Timothy Leary, Marcus Stellatus Palingenius, Sri Yukteswar, Vladimir Lenin, André Breton, William Shakespeare, Sir Francis Bacon, and the ancient scribes of Iceland. Apologies and thanks, as well, to the anonymous multitude who inadvertently wrote "One Hundred and Seventeen Steps."

Parts of "The Turbulated Curtain" were published in chapbook form as *The Sleepy Turbine* (LyricalMyrical Press, 2003). The fourth "Epistle," along with a line here and there, originally appeared in *Spiral Agitator* (Coach House Books, 2000). Other segments of this book have been published in or by *Surreal Estate: 13 Canadian Poets Under the Influence* (The Mercury Press, 2005), *The IV Lounge Reader* (Insomniac Press, 2001), *side/lines: A New Canadian Poetics* (Insomniac Press, 2002), *Oversion, CRASH, Unarmed, fhole, The New Chief Tongue* and THE EXPERT PRESS.

The phrase "That's not news, but that too is reality" was coined by the distinguished Canadian newscaster Peter Truman. "Moisturize into a firming glow" is a trademarked slogan of Jergens®.

As well as being an author, Steve Venright is a visual and sound artist whose Torpor Vigil Industries record label has released such remarkable CDs as *Songs of Elsewhere* by Samuel Andreyev and an album of spoken dreams called *The Further Somniloquies of Dion McGregor*. He was born in Sarnia in 1961 and now resides in a large consensual reality domain called Toronto, Ontario.

THESE CONFLUXIONS WERE MADE OF TEXTOPLASM
TO RESEMBLE HUMAN THOUGHT